To Whom Shall We Go?

TO WHOM SHALL WE GO?

Lessons from the Apostle Peter

CARDINAL
TIMOTHY M. DOLAN

Our Sunday Visitor Publishing Division
Our Sunday Visitor, Inc.
Huntington, Indiana 46750

Our Sunday Visitor Publishing Division
Our Sunday Visitor, Inc.
200 Noll Plaza
Huntington, IN 46750

ISBN: 978-1-59276-050-3 (Inventory No. T101)

LCCN: 2003113179

Cover design by Rebecca Heaston
Cover photo: Scala/Art Resource, NY
Interior design by Sherri L. Hoffman

PRINTED IN THE UNITED STATES OF AMERICA

DEDICATION

To my brother bishops, priests, and deacons,
the consecrated religious men and women,
and the wonderfully faithful people
of the Archdiocese of Milwaukee.

———

Jesus said to the twelve,
"Do you also wish to go away?"
Simon Peter answered him,
"Lord, to whom shall we go?
You have the words of eternal life;
and we have believed, and have come to know,
that you are the Holy One of God."

— JOHN 6:67-68

TABLE OF CONTENTS

Introduction   11

1. Keeping Our Eyes Focused on Christ:
   Matthew 14:22-33   19

2. "Noticing the Wind": Matthew 14:29-33   35

3. Silently Being with Our Lord: Mark 9:2-8   45

4. Embracing Our Cross: Matthew 16:21-24   61

5. How Do We Let God Love Us?: John 13:1-15   77

6. Do You Love the Lord?: John 21:15-17   91

7. *Duc in Altum* — "Put Out into the Deep":
   Luke 5:4-11   111

8. Asking Our Lord for Forgiveness: Mark 14:66-72   121

9. To Whom Shall We Go?: John 6:63-71   131

Afterword: Neither Silver Nor Gold: Acts 3:1-10   143

Introduction

In this book, St. Peter is our guide. By taking Scripture passages that relate incidents of the blessed apostle's life, usually with Jesus, we are able to draw valuable lessons on what it means to follow Our Lord. If you think about it — and I have a lot over the years — the words of St. Peter give us so much to reflect upon, and they are potent prayer starters. It is my hope that in reflecting with me upon these incidents from Peter's life, you will grow closer to him and, as a result, closer to Jesus.

Just think of some of the things Peter says — they are powerful prayers:

Lord, to whom shall we go? You alone have the words of everlasting life.

Lord, it's good to be here.

Lord, if it's really you, tell me to come to you across the water.

Save me, Lord, I'm drowning!

Leave me, Lord, for I am a sinful man.

Lord, wash not my feet only, but also my hands and my head!

You alone are the Christ, the Son of the Living God.

Lord, you know everything. You know that I love you.

I have no silver and gold, but I give you what I have; in the name of Jesus Christ of Nazareth, walk.

Peter, for all his clumsiness and sinfulness, all his cowardice and pride, is a tremendous example for us.

The Example of St. Peter

During my first year as rector of the North American College in Rome in 1994, we had a great spiritual director. So it was a surprise when one night he came to me in a panic and said, "Tim, I've got to resign."

I said, "Father, sit down. What's going on?"

"I have got to resign," he repeated. "I have just broken a student's confidence. I take that so seriously as a spiritual director that it's obvious that my integrity and my credibility will be destroyed, and I've got to quit. I've got to resign."

Now, I had already heard about the incident in question, a couple hours before, from another priest on the staff. What had happened was that this priest and this spiritual director were drying dishes in the faculty lounge and the priest had expressed a concern about a student. The spiritual director had, without any evil intent, revealed that the matter the other priest was worried about was, in fact, true. As the student's spiritual director, he could tell the other priest, "Don't worry about it. We're working on it. It's going to be all right." And, in an effort to reassure the other priest, he did so.

I also knew that prior to seeing me, the spiritual director had gone to see the student in question and apologized. The student had told him, "I don't know why you're upset. Don't even worry about it. There's nothing to worry about."

The "it" they were talking about wasn't any biggie — I mean it wasn't some graphic sexual thing or anything seriously immoral, only a relatively minor fault. But this priest was such a professional spiritual director that when he felt he had broken a student's confidence — even though the student had said that it was nothing to worry about — it devastated him to the point that he felt he had no choice but to resign.

I looked at him and said, "My friend, do me a favor. Let's take twenty-four hours and think about this. Why don't you take tomorrow off?" At that, I reached into my pocket and gave him my car keys. There weren't too many who had cars in Rome, but as the rector I had access to one. "Take the car," I continued, "and drive up to Assisi." I knew he loved Assisi, the town of St. Francis. "Leave early in the morning. Drive to Assisi. Spend the day there. Spend the night there if you wish. I'll pay for you. Bring me the bill. Just don't act rashly."

The spiritual director said, "Okay. I will."

The next day at lunch, unexpectedly, I saw him, and afterward he came to my office.

"Here are the car keys back," he said. "I didn't need to go up to Assisi. I was so upset I didn't even trust myself driving, so I simply walked over to St. Peter's Basilica. I went there early this morning, before any of the pilgrims were there. The place was empty." (If you go to St. Peter's in Rome before 9:00 in the morning, you discover its true purpose — it's a church, not a museum.) "I went to confession," he went on — which he could do because Franciscan confessors are available in the morning from 7:00 to 9:00 A.M. — "and after that, I simply went over to the tomb of St. Peter and spent some time in prayer. As I looked down to the altar of St. Peter over the apostle's tomb, I realized who was buried there and I thought, 'This guy denied Jesus three times at the moment when he needed him the most. This guy had committed a hideous sin, a terribly grievous sin, denied his best friend — the master, the savior of the world — three times. Yet this guy was the first to the empty tomb. This guy was the first to preach the Resurrection on Pentecost Sunday. This guy was the first pope. This guy came to Rome. This guy was the bishop of Rome. And upon the tomb of this man, crucified upside-down on this hill called the Vatican, rises up the greatest edifice in all of Christendom.'"

He went on, "Now, if Jesus can use this clumsy, sinful oaf named Peter and work such miracles and transform his person and his soul with such grace — well then, darn it, He can do it for me."

I will never forget him saying that.

Now, that's what I call an encounter with St. Peter, with the power of the example of St. Peter. The spiritual director allowed St. Peter to preach to him, and that's what I'd like to invite you to do as you read this book: allow the apostle Peter to be a living image of what God can do in your life.

"PLAY" ST. PETER

I'd like to quote from one of my favorites, Fr. Raymond Brown, who wrote a book about St. Peter. Here is how Raymond Brown described him:

> Peter. Here is a man who knew his lord so well that he could rise above his abundant weakness, impetuosity, cowardice, pride, anger, pettiness; accept the power and mercy of his master and become the first at the empty tomb, the premier apostle, the leader of the nation church, the rock upon which Christ built His church.

There is the power of St. Peter.

In this book, I am going to summon you to spend some time with St. Peter. I'm going to ask you to be next to him as he hears Jesus command, "Cast out into the deep." I'm going to invite you to be next to Peter:

- As he listens to the Master invite him to "Come follow me and I'll make you a fisher of men."

- As he chokes up when Jesus asks him not once, not twice, but three times, "Simon, do you love me?" and replies in exasperation, "Lord, you know everything. You know that I love you."
- As he reverses his stubbornness at the Last Supper and whispers, "Lord, wash not only my feet but my head and my hands, as well."
- As he's chastened severely by the Lord with the reprimand, "Get behind me, Satan!"
- As he falls at the feet of Christ and pleads, "Leave me, Lord, for I am a sinful man."
- As he professes, "You alone are the Christ, the Son of the Living God."
- As he dares Jesus, "Lord, if it's really you, tell me to come to you across the water," and then loses his faith and wails out, "Save me, Lord, I'm going to drown."
- As he responds to Our Lord's question if the disciples will leave him as well, "Lord, to whom shall we go? You alone have the words of everlasting life."
- As he says to the beggar in the temple square in Jerusalem, that first Pentecost, "Silver and gold I have not, but what I have I give you in the name of Jesus Christ, walk."

I always love the office of readings from the Liturgy of the Hours for the Feast of St. Thomas More, where we have the passage from the correspondence of Thomas More with his daughter, Margaret. Remember, Margaret had written him in the Tower of London and said, "Dad, please give up. Cave in. Do what the king wants. This isn't worth it. Save your life. We need you." And St. Thomas More writes back to his beloved daughter, Meg:

I will not mistrust Him, dear Meg, though I shall feel myself weakening and on the verge of being overcome by fear. I shall remember how St. Peter at a blast of wind began to sink because of his lack of faith, and I'll do as he did, call upon Christ and pray to Him for help, and then I trust He will place His holy hand upon me and in the stormy seas hold me up from drowning.

And if He permits me to play St. Peter further and to fall to the ground and to swear and forswear, may God our Lord in His tender mercy keep me from this, and let me lose if it so happen, and never win thereby!

That's what I'm asking you to do. Play St. Peter.

In his *Spiritual Exercises*, St. Ignatius of Loyola recommends that we contemplate Scripture. I'd like to paraphrase how he said we should contemplate:

First, take an episode from sacred Scripture. Take a scene from the gospels or any part of the Bible, and let your imagination go wild. Enter into it. Make the episode come alive by imagining you are there. Pretend you are part of it. (If you've ever made an Ignatian eight-day retreat or the thirty-day Spiritual Exercises, that's what you do. Your director will give you passages from sacred Scripture and, more or less, tells you to "contemplate on these" — which simply means to imagine that you're there.)

Second, pay attention to what happens. Who is in there? What are your sentiments? What are you saying to Jesus? What are you saying to Mary? What are you saying to the apostles? What are they saying to you?

That is what I'm asking you to do with this book, to use it as an aid to contemplation, in the way St. Ignatius taught us to contemplate — and to do it with St. Peter. In each chapter of this book, we'll look at a different episode that relates to Peter, a different event from the life of the prince of the apostles, and with him, we'll just try our best to grow as close to Jesus as he did.

1.

KEEPING OUR EYES FOCUSED ON CHRIST

Then [Jesus] made the disciples get into the boat and go before him to the other side, while he dismissed the crowds. And after he had dismissed the crowds, he went up into the hills by himself to pray. When evening came, he was there alone, but the boat by this time was many furlongs distant from the land, beaten by the waves; for the wind was against them. And in the fourth watch of the night he came to them, walking on the sea. But when the disciples saw him walking on the sea, they were terrified, saying, "It is a ghost!" And they cried out for fear. But immediately he spoke to them, saying, "Take heart, it is I; have no fear."

And Peter answered him, "Lord, if it is you, bid me come to you on the water." He said, "Come." So Peter got out of the boat and walked on the water and came to Jesus; but when he saw the wind, he was afraid, and beginning to sink he cried out, "Lord, save me." Jesus immediately reached out his hand and caught him, saying to him, "O man of little faith, why did you doubt?" And when they got into the boat, the wind ceased. And those in the boat worshiped him, saying, "Truly you are the Son of God."

— Mt. 14:22-33

Having a Firm Purpose

This has to be one of the more familiar episodes in the life of our hero, St. Peter. It contains so many nuggets of teaching and wisdom for us as we try our best to advance in the spiritual life. Just think of some of those prayers that we have from the mouth of St. Peter here: "Lord, if it is you, bid me come to you on the water," "Lord, save me." "Truly you are the Son of God." These are beautiful prayers that come from the lips of St. Peter and the other apostles.

The message — this is sledgehammer-clear — the message that Our Lord is trying to teach us in this famous episode: notice, as long as St. Peter keeps his eyes on Christ, he's doing fine. He can walk on water. The winds, the terrible storm, the ferocious waves, and the darkness don't bother him. But the moment he gets distracted, the moment he turns his gaze from the Lord, the moment Peter loses sight of his goal, what happens? He sinks!

That is a lesson that my little five-year-old niece could pick up — namely, as long as we keep our eyes locked on Christ, we'll be okay. The moment we avert our gaze from Him and begin to be consumed or distracted by something else, we're sunk. That's about as basic as you can get.

Steven Covey, one of the bestseller self-help gurus out there, has written several books and gives seminars on effective leadership and how to be happy and successful in life. Covey says that to be successful, you've got to have some very clear, simple goals. There can't be too many, but you set just a few goals. Then, come hell or high water, you keep your eyes on them and let nothing distract you. That seems obvious, but we know, from both our own and others' experiences, that most of the time we don't do it. One of two problems occurs — either we don't have the goals at all, or we set goals but then keep allowing distractions to take away our focus from them.

I remember once attending a lecture by one of the biographers of the late President of the United States, Ronald Reagan. The biographer noted that when he was going through the President's papers, he found a yellow sheet of paper — from one of those yellow legal pads — dated January 20, 1981, the day that Ronald Reagan was inaugurated President of the United States. The biographer could see that it had been around for a long time; the paper was folded and crumpled, as if Reagan had often unfolded it and looked at it. On that crumpled-up sheet from a legal pad, President Reagan had written down five goals — five goals for his presidency. Just five, but he kept them in front of him at all times. So, as the biographer said, like him or not, disagree with him or agree with him, people admire Ronald Reagan's leadership style because he was a man of simple goals and would not be distracted from them.

I propose to you that this Gospel passage (Mt. 14:22-33) would be suited right to Covey, and Reagan, because what it does is give us a very clear, attainable goal — namely, to keep our eyes riveted on Jesus. If we do that, no matter what waves, what storms, what lightning, or what darkness comes, we will not sink.

WALKING ON WATER

As long as St. Peter keeps his eyes riveted on Jesus . . . as long as the gaze of St. Peter is locked on the Master . . . as long as Peter keeps Jesus Christ as his one single goal . . . he can literally walk on water. But the moment he gets distracted, the moment he takes his eyes off Jesus, the moment he becomes aware of winds, waves, and storms around him, he gets afraid, and he begins to sink.

Look how basic a message of Christian discipleship this is. In our walk toward Jesus Christ, we are literally walking on water, no? To be a Christian today, to follow Our Lord, to accept His invitation to discipleship, really demands heroic courage. It really takes a miracle to stay close to Jesus and to live the kind of life He wants. He's asking us to walk on water.

Like St. Peter, Jesus is saying to us, "Come, come toward Me on the water."

Now, in our walk on water, the walk of Christian discipleship, as long as we keep our eyes riveted on Jesus, as long as Our Lord becomes our single goal, we can do the impossible! We can walk on the water toward Our Lord. But, the moment we get distracted, the moment we lose focus, the moment we begin to waver and take our eyes off Our Lord, we begin to sink.

I'd like to suggest some practical ways that we can keep our eyes locked on Christ, so that, like St. Peter, we can walk on the water toward Him.

How can we keep our eyes riveted on the Master? How can we keep looking at Jesus, beckoning us to walk on the water through life toward Him? One way is positive, the other more negative. Let's start with the positive way.

The Practice of the Presence of God
A way that we can, with St. Peter, keep our eyes focused on the Master, is by something I call (and I didn't make this up, this comes from the classical spiritual writers) "the practice of the presence of God."

The practice of the presence of God is a time-tried, beautifully effective, classical, and traditional Christian practice. What is it? It's really just another name for what we've been talking about — keeping our eyes on Jesus, aware constantly that the Lord is inviting us to walk on the water toward Him. How do we do it? There are a couple of ways that I find effective for practicing this presence of God.

The first is this: *to be ever conscious of the life of God within my soul*. We call this Sanctifying Grace, and I don't think we talk enough about it today.

I remember the first parish to which I was assigned back in the Archdiocese of St. Louis — Immacolata Parish, a great first assignment. Once while I was there, a young man came to me for instruction in the Catholic faith. He was a professor of mathematics at nearby Washington University. This guy was a tough convert. He was brilliant; he was an intellectual; he kind of fought me all along the way. He wanted to become a Catholic, but he was stubborn and wanted to argue a lot. We went through instructions in the faith for ten months and became good friends.

Finally, he said to me, "Father, I think I'm ready to become a Catholic, but I've got one thing I don't understand." Well, my mind began to race, as any priest will tell you, over the usual possibilities. I figured I could just about predict what his problem might be, because whenever a convert says there's something he doesn't understand, he or she usually means the role of the Holy Father, or maybe Purgatory, or maybe the special place that the Blessed Mother has in the Church, or the Real Presence of Our Lord in the Holy Eucharist, or the sacrament of Penance — one of those regular tenets of our faith that people coming into the Church have difficulty understanding. So, I was primed for my new convert to tell me which one of these was his problem.

"Go ahead," I invited. "Tell me, what's the thing you have trouble understanding?"

Was I ever surprised at his answer!

"Well, Father, way back in the beginning you talked to me about something called Sanctifying Grace. And I thought I heard you say that Sanctifying Grace means that the life of God actually lives in the soul of the believer. That the Blessed Trinity actually dwells in the soul of the believer. But I must have misunderstood you, because that is too good to be true."

Humbled, I replied the only way I could. "You understood me. You understood me perfectly. You have a beautiful appreciation of what Sanctifying Grace is all about."

It took that man, a man on his journey to become a Catholic, to teach me the awesome mystery of Sanctifying Grace.

So what does that mean to us? One of the ways, a practical way that we can practice the presence of God in our lives and unite with St. Peter in keeping our eyes riveted on Jesus, is by being constantly, gratefully, reverently, humbly aware of the gift of Sanctifying Grace. That the Lord actually lives in our soul, that we have dwelling within us the Blessed Trinity — that's what Sanctifying Grace is all about.

Cardinal Désiré Mercier was a great Scholastic philosopher who taught at the Catholic University of Louvain and, later, was made Archbishop of Malines, the provincial city of Belgium. There, he became a great patriot and a rallying point for the people of Belgium during the destruction, horror, and tragedy of the First World War. In the midst of Belgium's destruction, when the country was losing to the advance of the Kaiser and everything had been destroyed, Mercier wrote a pastoral letter that was read in all the churches throughout the country. The letter was about what they needed to do to rebuild the country, what they needed to hang onto in order to keep hope.

In that letter, Cardinal Mercier said, "First things first." Talking as a father to a people so devastated from the war, he said, "Every day, I want you simply to close your eyes and enter the sanctuary of your baptized soul, and there realize that God Himself dwells."

That's what I call practicing the presence of God. That's what I call keeping our eyes locked on Christ. "Every day I want you simply to close your eyes and enter the sanctuary of your baptized soul, and there realize that God Himself dwells." And those words, of course, galvanized the people of Belgium and gave them the courage and hope that they needed to rise above the ashes.

Tell me how — if we are reverently, gratefully, humbly aware of the gift of Sanctifying Grace, the life of God in our soul — how we could be anything *but* conscious of the presence of God. How could we be anything *but* walking on the water with St. Peter toward Jesus? We could face the waves and winds around us without fear, knowing that God is with us!

So there's one way — constant consciousness of grace within us.

PRAYING IN THE PRESENCE OF THE LORD — ADORATION
A second way that we can practice the presence of God, and therefore keep our eyes locked on Christ, would be the Eucharist. For me as a priest, of course, the Eucharist — the celebration of the Mass — is not just part of the day; it is "the heart of the day," to use a little phrase of which Cardinal Richard Cushing was very fond. For all of us, the Eucharist is a potent way to literally lock our eyes on Christ.

I remember once at a gathering of candidates for the seminary, with about twenty young men present, we opened it up to their questions. Predictably, one of them asked, "How do you guys handle all of the scandals and all of the difficulties and problems that the Church has today?" One of our priests answered.

"Every day at Mass," he said, "I have the honor of lifting up the Body of Christ to the people at the consecration, and I hold it up to them to look at Him and adore Him. And at that moment I picture myself as a priest, not only holding up Christ — but I picture Christ holding me up. Jesus is my support. He is the one that sustains me. He is the one that gives me strength."

What this priest was saying, of course, is that for him, the Eucharist was a very potent way to keep his eyes locked on Christ, a very practical way to practice the presence of God.

I'm very fond of Henri Nouwen. There was a study just completed about the three priests who had greatest impact on priests ordained after the Second Vatican Council. The three were Karl Rahner, Andrew Greeley, and Henri Nouwen.

I was privileged to spend a semester with Henri Nouwen when I was a student and he was a scholar in residence with us in Rome. I didn't know at the time that Henri Nouwen had battled with depression for a good chunk of his life. There is a powerful passage in one of his biographies that talks about a particularly low point in Nouwen's life, when he was really questioning his vocation to the priesthood. At that point, desperately trying to find a purpose and an assurance of God's love and mercy, he felt like he had tried everything. He went to psychotherapy. He made a thirty-day retreat. He received intense spiritual direction.

It was while Nouwen was exploring the Eastern mystical approaches in India that he had a chance meeting with Mother Teresa in Calcutta, and he poured out his heart and soul to her. When he had finished, Mother Teresa, in her characteristically simple way, said, "Father, you are so anxious and so desperate to find purpose and to find meaning, to find a goal in your life. Do you ever purposely hurt anyone?"

Nouwen said, "Mother, I'm sure I've hurt people. But I'd never do it on purpose."

"Fine. Do you celebrate the Holy Mass every day?"

"Mother, I have throughout my priesthood, every day, unless I've been sick or unless something that I can't help came up."

"Well, you're doing fine. What's the big deal?" Mother Teresa said. "You're not purposely hurting any of God's people, and every day you're uniting yourself with Christ on the cross in that great prayer. Drop it. Quit your search. I think you're doing just fine."

Nouwen's biographer said that that was a turning point in the priests's life, he was so moved by that simplicity. While he had been so frantically and desperately searching for some focus and meaning, Mother Teresa had simply pointed out that in the Eucharist, we've got our goal. What do you keep running around the world looking for? You've got the eyes of Christ right there.

STAYING FOCUSED ON CHRIST — PRAYER

A third way that we can practice the presence of God, a positive way for us to keep our eyes riveted on Jesus in our walk of faith across the water toward Him, is prayer. I'm talking about the kind of prayer that Cardinal John Henry Newman spoke of as *cor ad cor loquitur*, "heart speaking to heart." Let me ramp that up a bit, because the kind of prayer I'm speaking about here is not so much heart speaking to heart, but eyes to eyes. That's a good way to pray. It's sometimes a frightening way to pray — to picture ourselves staring into the face of Christ, to imagine the eyes of Jesus looking back into us.

There is a point in a wedding ceremony where the priest will say to the couple, "Now turn to one another for your vows," and very often he'll whisper, "Look at each other." You know, "Look into one another . . ." The woman usually doesn't have a problem with this, but the guy's sort of looking at his watch and what are his ushers doing, and, well, you get the idea that it's tough to look into somebody's eyes. That is what I'm asking you to consider, prayer in the way that I'm talking about it — as staring into the eyes of Christ, and letting Him stare at you while you gaze at Him.

You will notice when you read the Gospel that we often hear about Christ looking intently at someone — for example, Our Lord's encounter with the rich young man. Remember in Mark's Gospel in Chapter 10, verses 17-22? The rich young man comes and asks Jesus what he must do to inherit eternal life, and Jesus tells him. Then there is a moving passage: "Jesus looking upon him loved him" (Mk. 10:21). Another episode talks about Peter, after he had denied Jesus three times in the Temple courtyard: "And the Lord turned and looked at Peter" (Lk. 22:61).

Pope John Paul II, in his Apostolic Letter *Novo Millennio Ineunte* (*On the Close of the Great Jubilee Year 2000*), encouraged a renewed devotion to contemplating the face of Christ. Although this devotion has always been around, it seems to be not only gaining popularity in the Church today but needed in a special way: a devotion to the face of Christ, spending time picturing the face of Jesus.

A phenomenally successful exhibit on St. Peter and the popes traveled throughout the United States a few years ago. When it came to Milwaukee, one of the curators at the museum told me that the most popular piece in the exhibit was the *Mandylion* — the image of Our Lord's face on a veil, also called the Image of Edessa. The story behind this veil is that the king of Edessa, who was dying, had heard about the healings of Jesus and sent some of his people to beg the Lord to come to him. Jesus did not go to him, but gave the people a cloth that He pressed to His face, leaving His image impressed upon it. The people took the image back to the king of Edessa, and when he touched the cloth, he was cured. I don't know if that's true or not. But as the Italians say, "If it's not true, it ought to be." What we do know for sure is that the cloth dates back to about the fifth century and is one of the earliest claimed impressions of the face of Jesus Christ.

The curator of the museum told me that when people came to the *Mandylion*, the Image of Edessa, they would just stop in their tracks and stare at it. He would often see people in tears as they contemplated the face of Christ. This is what I'm proposing that we do — in union with St. Peter, look into the face of Christ, letting His eyes look upon us. And if we do that in our prayer, just close our eyes and picture Jesus looking at us and us staring back, I contend that this kind of prayer is a great example of the *via positiva*, the positive way to practice the presence of Christ.

All prayer, of course, is linked to our ability to stay focused on Christ. Prayer is precisely keeping our eyes locked on Jesus. A very practical way to continue to walk on the water toward Christ is by being fervent and faithful in our prayer. Prayer is the way that we practice the presence of God.

SR. MARY BOSCO'S THREE ALL-IMPORTANT PRAYERS

When I was in second grade, I had a great teacher, Sr. Mary Bosco. Way back then, Sister told me something, and it is something that I have never forgotten. It is great counsel and has gotten me through a lot. She gave me three simple prayers to be said upon rising, during the day, and at night. She said, "If you don't do anything else during the day, at least say these three prayers.

"When you get up in the morning, you should make a good Morning Offering and say your other prayers, but the least you should do is simply say, 'All for Thee, Most Sacred Heart of Jesus,' devoting the entire day to the Lord." *All for Thee, Most Sacred Heart of Jesus.*

Then she added, "During the day, whenever there are moments of difficulties, or moments of temptation, or moments of adversity, or moments of sorrow, or moments of challenge, you say, 'Sacred Heart of Jesus, I place all my trust in Thee,' asking the help of the Lord.

"Then at night, if you do nothing more, at least before you go to bed, you say, 'Most Sacred Heart of Jesus, have mercy on me, a sinner,' asking the Lord's pardon for whatever you may have done during the day to offend Him."

That's what I call the practice of the presence of God through prayer. Very simple, very practical, keeping our eyes focused on the Lord. *All for Thee, Most Sacred Heart of Jesus. Sacred Heart of Jesus, I place all my trust in Thee. Most Sacred Heart of Jesus, have mercy on me, a sinner.*

SIMPLE REMINDERS

One Tuesday some years ago, when I was in Rome taking a visitor on a tour of the Vatican, we met an American priest while going through the offices of the Secretary of State. In the course of our conversation, he mentioned, "I've got to get back to work because I'm translating the Pope's general audience address for tomorrow into English." At his desk, I noticed that he had a document from Pope John Paul II, handwritten in Polish.

I asked, "Can I see that?"

He was gracious enough to allow me to hold it — so there I was, holding the Pope's handwritten text in Polish. I'm showing it to my friends and what do I notice? At the top of the page is written *A-M-D-G*, in the pope's very own hand. *A-M-D-G*. Those who were educated by the Jesuits probably know what that means. Those letters stand for *Ad Majorem Dei Gloriam*, a Latin phrase that means "To the Greater Glory of God."

What was Pope John Paul II doing in writing those four letters *A-M-D-G*? He was making his work a simple prayer that kept him focused on the Lord.

That is what this is all about, keeping our eyes riveted on the Master — the practice of the presence of God. You don't have to be a contemplative for that. You don't have to be a cloistered sister. All of us practice the presence of God. All of us keep our eyes focused on the Master through these simple, moving, practical prayers during the day.

When I was in the seminary, the Archbishop of St. Louis was Cardinal John Carberry, who told us that every time he answered the phone, he would say a little aspiration beforehand to ask for Our Lord's help. I remember at the time — I'm embarrassed to say — that we kind of giggled, and thought. "Oh, this is some pious practice." No, it's not! You talk about down-to-earth? You talk about practical? This is a man who practiced the presence of God. This is a man, like St. Peter, who is trying to keep his gaze focused on Jesus by practicing the presence of God in a very fundamental way.

LITURGY OF THE HOURS

We priests, and an ever growing number of laity as well, have a very powerful way in our daily prayer to practice the presence of Christ: the Liturgy of the Hours.

I was blessed, very blessed as a kid. My dad dropped dead when he was fifty-one, but I remember somebody coming up to me at his wake and saying, "You know, Tim, your mom and dad were still like teenagers in love." And they were very much so, as I think back now with immense gratitude.

One of the things my dad would do every day — and I can remember as a kid seeing my mom giggle at this — is to write notes before he left for work early in the morning and put them around the house, where Mom would find them throughout the day.

So, for instance, my mom would open up the freezer door and see a note that he had just snuck in there, on the meat that she was going to get out to thaw. It would say, "Honey, I love you. See you soon."

Throughout the day, my dad would keep in touch with mom to express his love; that's sort of what we do when we pray the Liturgy of the Hours. We're keeping in touch with the presence of God. We're locking our eyes on Jesus Christ.

I am reminded of an incident that Cardinal Theodore McCarrick related to me from his time as Archbishop of Newark, NJ, about awaiting the arrival of Pope John Paul II.

Archbishop McCarrick is waiting with all the priests, all the security, all the policemen, ready to begin the motorcade to 100,000 people in Giants Stadium, as the helicopter carries Pope John Paul II from Manhattan — he had been in New York City — over the river to Newark. They're running late, it's pouring rain, and he's really eager to get the Holy Father there.

At last, the helicopter lands, and some of the papal party come out . . . but no Pope. One minute, two minutes, three minutes, still no Pope. At this point, Archbishop McCarrick starts getting nervous, turns to the Holy Father's Secretary, and says, "Where's the Holy Father?"

The Secretary just smiles. "He's praying Evening Prayer. He is saying his Office and there is no rushing him."

Now, that's what I mean by practicing the presence of God. That is what I mean by prayer keeping us focused on Jesus. We need very practical times during the day that we refocus our eyes on Jesus.

TRUST IN THE LORD

What I propose to you is that every time you pray, you hear Jesus say, as he did to St. Peter, "Take heart, it is I; have no fear." That every morning when you get up, you hear Jesus saying to you: "Come. Walk across the water toward me." Following Christ in this life is nothing less than walking across the water toward Christ. We cannot do it on our own. We will sink unless we keep our eyes locked on Him. In this chapter, I've tried to give you a few ways that can help us do this in a positive way, by keeping our eyes locked on Jesus.

One of the great Fathers of the Church, Gregory of Nyssa, says:

> We shall be blessed with clear vision if we keep our eyes fixed on Christ. St. Paul himself, and all who have reached heights of sanctity, had their eyes fixed on Christ and so have all who live and move and have their being in him. As no darkness can be seen by anyone surrounded by light, so no trivialities can capture the attention of anyone who has his eyes on Christ. The one who keeps his eyes upon the head and origin of the whole universe has them on virtue and all its perfection. He has them on truth, on justice, on immortality, and on everything else that is good, for Christ is goodness itself. See the things that are above, which is only another way of saying — keep your eyes on Christ.

2.

"Noticing the Wind"

So Peter got out of the boat and walked on the water and came to Jesus; but when he saw the wind, he was afraid, and beginning to sink he cried out, "Lord, save me." Jesus immediately reached out his hand and caught him, saying to him, "O man of little faith, why did you doubt?" And when they got into the boat, the wind ceased. And those in the boat worshiped him, saying, "Truly you are the Son of God."

— Mt. 14:29-33

Staying Afloat

What dominates in your life?

Now you might wonder, what do I mean by that? Let me state it another way: What are the waves and the winds in your life that can periodically threaten to sink you?

St. Peter had a bunch of them. St. Peter had a lot of waves and winds in his life. When he's walking on the water, no wonder he gets distracted. The waves are lapping up, the winds are coming on strong, and there he is, out in the middle of a very large lake.

What are the waves and the winds in your life that can tempt you to take your eyes off Christ? We've all got them. So, what dominates in your life?

I use that word "dominate" on purpose, because, you know, *dominate* comes from the same word as *Dominus,* the Latin word for "Lord." So, really, what I am asking you is

"What 'lords' over your life? What dominates your life? Who is Lord of your life?"

Is it Jesus? Or is it the waves and the winds that seem to threaten to sink you?

In Chapter 1, I suggested positive ways to keep our eyes locked on Christ. Now we must consider the *via negativa*: what are the winds and waves that distract us from the goal of Christ?

Taking Inventory of Our Lives

One of the best things we can do in our Christian life is to ask ourselves with brutal honesty:

- What is it in my life that threatens to destroy me?
- What are the sins?
- What are the bad habits?
- What are the worries?
- What are the temptations?
- What things are bothering me?
- What things so get to me and so disrupt me, and so distract me that I take my eyes off the Lord and begin to sink?

Now, we've all got them! There is something in our life that weighs on us. There are things that threaten to capsize us. There is some wind or wave in our life that so distracts us that we remove our gaze from Christ and begin to sink. One of the best things we can do is ask ourselves these questions, and keep asking them — because nothing else but the Lord can truly dominate us if we trust in Jesus Christ, who must be our constant focus.

So here is a first practical way that we can kind of keep our eyes focused on Christ: simply ask ourselves, "What dominates me? What are the winds and the waves in my life that threaten to overwhelm me?" Then, when we find ourselves in that predicament — when we find ourselves like St. Peter when those waves and those winds, when those forces, when those anxieties, when those sins, when those difficulties, when those vices tend to beg us to look their way — then, with St. Peter, we cry out to Jesus, "Save me, Lord. I'm going to drown."

An Examination of Conscience

One of the most practical things we can do in our walk on the water toward Our Lord is to identify — with all the humility and candor that we've got at our disposal — what it is that threatens to drown us. Once we know that, once we know the things that threaten to capsize us, then we can be aware of them, keep them under control, not let them knock us off course, and continue to keep our gaze riveted on the Master.

Really, what we're asking is:

- What are the sins in my life?
- What are the unredeemed areas?
- Where is the realm of darkness still outside the redeeming power of Christ?
- What are the troubles and the problems and the distractions and anything in my life that can sink me and threaten to take my gaze off that of Jesus?

Now, most of us have been around long enough to know what these things are, and I'm not asking you to be obsessed with them. I'm simply saying that if we're going to be realistically spiritual — if we're going to be successful in our quest for holiness, which is what life is all about — well, then, we'd better be real when it comes to knowing our dark side, the things that can sink us and get to us. You know in your own spiritual journey that Jesus is always inviting us to come to Him, and as we come closer to Him, there is always something to turn away from.

Mother Teresa had a beautiful line in which she said we will detect the finger of Christ in two areas of our life. Most of the time, He's looking at us and beckoning us to come closer to Him. But there are also times He's behind us, tapping us on the back and saying, "Turn around and come back to Me." As the great Fathers of the Church taught, growth in sanctity always means turning *toward* something — namely, Christ — and turning *away from* something else— namely, sin, our own dark side.

So what are the winds, waves, and darkness in our lives? Our hero, St. Peter, sure had a lot of them. As he's walking on the water toward Our Lord, he literally has waves, thunder and lightning, and darkness competing with Our Lord for his attention — not to mention the fact that it probably entered into his mind that as a human, he shouldn't be able to walk on the water! But he also had figurative storms in his life, those spiritual clouds that periodically dominated him, taking his eyes off of Christ and leaving him to sink. I'm thinking, for instance, of pride.

"Oh, Lord, all these others might desert you, but not me. Not me." Remember that one, at the Last Supper? There was pride. That was a spiritual storm in the life of Peter.

There was selfishness. "Lord, we've left everything to follow you. What's in it for me?" Selfishness was another dark side.

There was temper. Remember Peter cut off the ear of the high priest's servant, earning the stern rebuke of the Master?

There was cowardice, as he caved in out of fear to those very non-threatening people in the courtyard that night of Our Lord's Passion and denied his Master three times.

Those were some of the moral and spiritual "clouds, waves, and winds" that got to Peter and would threaten to sink him.

Those were St. Peter's. I'm going to propose that we had better know ours, as well.

St. John Vianney wrote that the man of sanctity is even more conscious of the dark side of himself than he is of the grace and mercy of the Lord. So the only way we can move toward the Lord is by being very realistically conscious of the things that will sink us.

I find a good way to examine my conscience, especially in preparation for the sacrament of Penance, is to picture myself walking on the water toward Christ, then picture the winds and the waves around me that are taking me away from him, and to tag those, to name those. Another way to do this is to ask who or what has dominion in my life, other than Jesus Christ?

SELF-POSSESSION

I had only been in Rome as Rector of the North American College a month or two when a visitor came unannounced. It was the archbishop of Seattle, a Chicagoan by the name of Thomas Murphy, who since has died, Lord have mercy on him. Archbishop Murphy was a fairly renowned rector in his day and had also been rather instrumental in writing one of the drafts of the program of priestly formation. One hot Roman day, in the middle of summer, I can remember asking him, "Archbishop, what advice have you got for me? You've been a seminary rector a long time. What do I need to talk to future priests about?"

Without missing a beat, Archbishop Murphy said, "Make sure your guys are self-possessed men."

I hadn't heard that term before. "What do you mean by 'self-possessed'?"

"I mean a guy who knows what he's about," the archbishop replied. "A man who knows his strengths and his weaknesses, a guy who acknowledges that he's loved passionately by a God who will never let him down, a man who's confident in his priestly vocation and identity, secure enough to weather the storms, a guy who's not swayed by emotions and passions or difficulties, humble enough to every day ask God's help, so mature in his faith that he can give himself selflessly to his people without needing rewards right now. That's what I mean by a self-possessed man."

I've never forgotten that definition. Peter was self-possessed as long as he kept his eyes on Christ. Once he lost possession of his goal, of his Christ, and of himself, that's when he sank.

Certain attributes come to mind when I think of self-possession: strength, confidence, maturity, humility, sturdiness, simplicity, and sincerity. I think, for instance, of someone like Pope John Paul II, a self-possessed man. Who can ever forget when he was standing there on a return visit to Poland in the presence of the then-head of the Polish Communist Party, General Jaruzelski — who had hundreds of thousands of troops to back him up there in his military outfit. And there stands the pope next to him, who has nothing from a physical, materialistic point of view. Was he going to send sixty Swiss guards to liberate Poland? He has no currency to float or troops to send. Yet it's Jaruzelski whose knees are knocking and who is shaking as he holds the paper he reads from, and it's Pope John Paul II who just stands there in complete self-possession. The pope knew what he was about. He was dominated by no one except his Lord, his faith, and his sense of his own identity.

When I speak of a self-possessed man, of course, I also think of Jesus himself: confident in His identity as the only-begotten son of the Father; firm in His pursuit to redeem humanity, even when He knew it would lead to His passion and cross; unflinching in the fulfillment of His vocation; undistracted by the ranting of the mob for a "bread king," the reasoning of our friend Peter trying to talk Him out of the cross, or by the trepidation of sweat so intense that it turned into blood. He was self-possessed in truth before Pilate's waffling, self-possessed by love before the hateful jeers of the crowd, and self-possessed by His sense of mercy and forgiveness in the face of hate and violence of His tormentors. That is a self-possessed man.

WHAT DOMINATES US

Another term that I like is "domination." Fr. Michael Scanlan, the former president of the University of Steubenville, is a Franciscan writer and speaker who reminds us that this word comes from the Latin *dominus*. *Dominus*, of course, meaning "lord." So Fr. Scanlan says, "When we ask ourselves who or what dominates our life, who or what is sovereign in our life, who or what has absolute authority in our life, is it the *dominus*"— the Lord, Our Lord and Savior Jesus Christ — "or is it someone or something else?"

Fr. Scanlon asks us: Is Jesus lord in our life? Is Jesus the *dominus*? Does He dominate? Or does someone or something else dominate our life? Is it worry, anxiety, anger, hurt, wealth, alcohol, vengeance? It could be Satan, our possessions, or another person. It could be myriad things. But it boils down to the fact that only the *dominus*, only the Lord God, should dominate. If anything else dominates, something is out of kilter in our life.

You could rephrase it: as Peter walks on the water, who is going to dominate? Jesus, as Peter keeps his eyes locked on Him, or the winds and the waves around him? If the storm dominates, he literally sinks. So with Peter we make an act of faith in Jesus Christ — you and you alone are the son of God, you alone are the Christ, the Son of the Living God. What a meaningful act of faith! What Peter's saying is — and remember what the context is here — (Mt. 16:13-16), is that all those other opinions and theories, they don't dominate. The only thing that dominates is my faith that you and you alone are the Christ, the Son of the Living God.

That statement has moral implications. What we're saying is that money, property, ambition, anger, lust, drink, immoral relationships, obsessions, gambling, whatever it is — it can't dominate. It can't be lord of our lives. Only Christ — you and you alone are the Son of God in my life. You are the *dominus*. You alone dominate, as I keep my eyes locked on you. It's another version of the First Commandment, "I am the LORD your God, who brought you out of the land of Egypt, out of the house of bondage. You shall have no other gods before me."

I remember when I was a child in sixth grade and Sr. Gemma warned us, "Fr. Callahan, the pastor, is coming, and he expects you all to know the Ten Commandments," so we memorized the Ten Commandments in preparation for his coming. Well, Fr. Callahan came in and sure enough, he said, "Who's going to tell me the Ten Commandments?" I guess I was waving my hand the most, because he called on me. So I stood up and said, "I am the Lord thy God, thou shalt not have strange gods before me. Second Commandment . . ."

And I went blank.

I only knew the first, and I was ready for the wrath of the pastor. But instead, he only said, "Well, that's not bad. In a way, that's the most important." And it is, obviously; if we know that He is the Lord, He is God, and we have no strange gods and nothing else dominates, that's probably the most important commandment. No wonder it is first. "I am the LORD your God, you shall have no other gods before me." Nobody else dominates.

Gregory the Great speaks poetically about the man who masters himself, who is dominated only by Christ:

> The man possessed by Christ bears wrongs with equanimity, shows his kindness by generously repaying good for evil. Jealousy is foreign to him. It's impossible to envy worldly success when he has no worldly desires. He is not conceited. The prize he covets is within. He's not ambitious. The welfare of his own soul is what he cares about. Apart from that, he seeks nothing. He is not selfish. Unable to keep anything anyway. He's indifferent to it as if it were in others. He is not quick to take offense. Even under provocation thoughts of revenge never cross his mind. The reward he seeks hereafter will be greater in proportion to his endurance. He harbors no evil thoughts. Hatred is utterly rooted out of a heart whose only love is goodness. Thoughts that defile a man can find no entry. He does not gloat over other people's sins or misfortunes. He only longs for his and their salvation.

There is a man who has Jesus as his *dominus* and is dominated by no other sin or passion, no evil desire, or wind, or wave, or storm.

Be Prepared for the Storms

So I ask you to tag the things that distract you, call out to you, and move you away from the Lord in our lives. I know mine. I think you all know yours. What scares me is that there are other waves in my life of which I'm not aware. Those are the ones that can hurt us, aren't they? Those are the ones that can topple us. The ones we know, at least we've tagged and we've submitted to the mercy and grace of God. The ones we don't know, either because of pride or ignorance, those are the ones that can sink us. Those are the waves that can do us in.

The other thing we all learn is that there might be a given time when we are able to let go of something that dominates us, other than Jesus. We can take care of it and submit it and get over it, but guess what? Something always comes in to take its place, right? There is always going to be a wind, a wave, a storm to threaten us to take our eyes off Jesus, so we must be constantly, constantly vigilant.

When we're aware of all those things that can get to us and sink us, then we are ready to say with St. Peter, aware of our weakness, "You and you alone are the Christ, the Son of the Living God. You and you alone dominate. No one and nothing else because, Lord, I am possessed not by Satan or this world. I am possessed by you and by a sense of self that you have given me because of the way I live now — not I, but you live in me."

3.

SILENTLY BEING WITH OUR LORD

And after six days Jesus took with him Peter and James and John, and led them up a high mountain apart by themselves; and he was transfigured before them, and his garments became glistening, intensely white, as no fuller on earth could bleach them. And there appeared to them Elijah with Moses; and they were talking to Jesus. And Peter said to Jesus, "Master, it is well that we are here; let us make three booths, one for you and one for Moses and one for Elijah." For he did not know what to say, for they were exceedingly afraid. And a cloud overshadowed them, and a voice came out of the cloud, "This is my beloved Son; listen to him." And suddenly looking around they no longer saw any one with them but Jesus only.

— Mk. 9:2-8

THE TRANSFIGURATION

In this incident of the Transfiguration, I am moved by what Peter did *not* say. This is one of the few times in which the Gospel tells us that Peter didn't know what to say. He simply says, "Lord, it is good that we are here with You." Listen closely to those words. It's almost as if this very hyperactive, impetuous St. Peter simply wanted to savor being quietly in the presence of the Master, to enjoy the person of Jesus and remain silent.

I remember once, when I was rector of the North American College in Rome — and pardon me for having so many stories from there, but I got to know so many great people there. One of them was the late, great Archbishop of New York, John Cardinal O'Connor, who had come over to Rome for some final business when he knew he was dying. On one particular evening he was speaking, reflecting upon his life, and I remember asking him, "Your Eminence, is there anything in your life that you really regret?" Without a moment's hesitation, he said, "I talked too much. I should have been quiet much more often."

He went on, "When I came to New York, they were always sticking microphones in my face. They were always asking for comments. I took the bait all the time. And more often than not, had I simply kept my mouth shut, I would have been in much better shape."

Now to St. Peter. He was so awestruck he did not know what to say. There again is the wisdom, the power, of silence. Peter teaches us a pivotal lesson in the spiritual life: a powerful, effective way to intensify union with the Lord is by simply being with Him in silence. We're talking about the power of *being*. We're talking about the power of silence.

Simply Being

In his great pastoral exhortation, *Pastores dabo vobis* (a document that was directed to seminaries in priestly formation), Pope John Paul II makes a significant distinction. In the opening pages, he says that the great temptation of contemporary life is to concentrate on "having and doing, instead of being."

Let me repeat the Holy Father's words: "The great temptation is to concentrate on having and doing, instead of being."

I'm reminded of Fr. Bill Byron's statement: "You know, we are human *beings,* not human *doings.*" He had the same sense that the Holy Father did — that much more important than having, much more important than doing, is simply the primacy of being.

At that very pivotal moment in the rite of ordination when a candidate to be ordained comes forward — here, in many ways, the climax of that person's life — what does the Church ask the priestly candidate to do? Years of discernment, years of preparation, years of getting ready, years of being found worthy, years of preparation . . . and at that sacred moment, the Rite of Ordination simply has that young deacon, priest, or bishop-to-be simply say — what?

"Present."

That's all. He doesn't stand up and say, "I'm ready. I'm prepared. I'm worthy. I'm enthusiastic. I deserve this." The Church simply has the candidate say, "Present."

Present. That's all we can do, is *be* there. There is nothing much we can say. Nothing much to do. A man certainly can't earn ordination, achieve it, or win it. All he can do is simply give Our Lord his presence. He can just be with Him. There it is again, the power of being. The power of silence.

When you think about it, Christ himself came to the world in silence, the silence of a Judean night. Christ redeemed the world in silence. The silence of the lamb, dumb before its shearer. And Christ comes to our hearts now, preferentially, in silence.

We certainly have our work cut out for us! Because we prefer — I prefer, something tells me you prefer, our culture prefers, our world prefers, our society prefers — having, doing, clutter, and noise. We prefer all that over being, presence, and quiet.

The Cistercian poet Jan Walgrave cautions us, "You must remember that the contemporary world represents a conspiracy against the silence necessary for the interior life."

"Lord, it is good that we are here with You." Thank you, St. Peter!

When you think about it, every day is a time to be with Jesus. We usually think of growing spiritually in terms of doing more things for the Lord, and there is a indeed a value in that. But I invite you to take a good example from St. Peter and simply concentrate on being with Jesus, being present.

"Lord, it is good that we are here with You."

How can we concentrate on simply being with Jesus? I propose to you that there are two practical ways to accomplish this.

THE FIRST WAY — PRAYER

The first is going to come as no surprise: prayer. Prayer is a way we can, with St. Peter, say, "Lord, it is good to be here with You."

We usually think of prayer as saying things to Our Lord, and there's certainly that aspect of prayer — when we tell Him we love Him, when we tell Him what we need, when we tell Him we are sorry for our sin, when we praise and thank Him. Yes, prayer is saying things to Jesus. But I suggest we not forget that prayer is also a time to be with Jesus.

Is there anything more eloquent than silence, than just being in somebody's presence? When I was a new priest, I used to go to a nursing home on Saturdays. I would visit a lady there who obviously had dementia, probably Alzheimer's (although they didn't even call it Alzheimer's back in 1976, when I was ordained). She just lay in bed and stared. Her husband was always there every Saturday that I would go with Holy Communion, and I so admired his tenderness with her. He would sit with her, hold her hands, speak to her, and get nothing from her. Nothing. The husband even told me once, "Father, she hasn't said a word. There has not been a look of recognition for nine years." Yet daily he was there, so loyal, just being with her.

And I remember going to the wake when she died. I've never seen a man so distraught. I've never seen a man sadder than that husband. I saw him crying and went up to give him my condolences.

"I'm going to miss her so much," was all he could say. I thought to myself, *He's going to miss her presence.* He wasn't going to miss her words, because she hadn't said anything for nine years — but the power of presence, the power of just silently *being* with somebody, sometimes is so eloquent that you don't even need words.

Think about it. Think of the words in the Gospel that Jesus uses when He invites His disciples to come to Him. He doesn't use action words, does He? He doesn't say "Work with Me." He doesn't say "Act with Me." He doesn't say "Exercise with Me" (thank God!). He doesn't say "Run with Me." He doesn't say "Organize with Me." He doesn't say "Produce things with Me. Do things with Me." No! What does Jesus say when He's addressing His disciples and us in the Gospel?

Listen closely. The words that Our Lord uses are: "Abide with Me." "Remain with Me." "Be with Me." "Stay awake with Me." "Live with Me." "Watch with Me."

I mentioned to you that prayer is a way that we can be with Jesus; I want to get specific with you and mention some different ways of prayer that really help us to be with Jesus.

PRAYING IN THE PRESENCE OF OUR LORD
First, there is prayer before the Holy Eucharist.

Do you remember the beautiful story about St. John Vianney, the Curé of Ars? He would pray every day. He would just kneel in silence before Our Lord in the Blessed Sacrament for an hour, an hour and a half, two hours. And his parishioners would gather around and they would look at him with curiosity when he had just come into the Village of Ars.

Finally, one of them got up the courage and said, "Father, what do you say to Jesus all that time?"

And the Curé of Ars, St. John Vianney, answered. He said, "I don't say anything. I look at Him. He looks back at me."

Being with Jesus . . . "Lord, it is good that we are here with You."

I remember on September 11, 2001, coming back after that horribly long, dark, sad day to the rectory of Our Lady of Sorrows Parish, a great parish in South St. Louis. In that parish we had a chapel, next door to the rectory, where people could come and spend time in prayer before the Blessed Sacrament. As I'm getting out of the car ready to go into the rectory, I decide to make a visit to the chapel. At that moment, here comes this young mother with her two children, and she says to me, "Bishop, I figure I can either stay at home and look at CNN, or come up here and look at Him."

That young mother knew what we're talking about. She knew that simply to be with Jesus in that moment of national sorrow was very effective. Jesus is really and truly present in the Blessed Sacrament — Body, Blood, Soul, and Divinity — and it is good just to be with Him. Sometimes we struggle with things to say, sometimes we're discouraged, sometimes we're confused, sometimes we're down in the dumps, words don't come easy. So what? At that time before Our Lord in the

Eucharist, it is good to say, like St. Peter, "Lord, it is good to be here with You."

I remember when I was first ordained and we had the Altar of Repose on Holy Thursday. People would sign up for periods of prayer from nine to twelve in the evening to spend time with Our Lord in the Holy Eucharist. I was responsible for leading the last hour of the evening.

I'm a new priest, running around thinking, "Should I read from the Scriptures? Should we do some psalms? Should I lead the Sorrowful Mysteries of the Rosary? Should I do the Stations of the Cross? What should I do?" And I asked one of the older sisters, Sr. Ludmilla, "Sister, what should I do during this Holy Hour before Our Lord in the Holy Eucharist?"

Do you know what Sr. Ludmilla told me? She replied, "Father, let's just have silence. Let's just be with Our Lord." She knew what St. Peter was saying, "Lord, it is good to be here with You."

So, there's one practical way to be with Jesus — silent prayer before Our Lord really and truly present in the Blessed Sacrament.

PRAYING THE GOSPELS

A second way to be with Our Lord is through reverent reading of the Gospels. In classical spiritual theology, we call this *lectio divina*, which is spiritual reading — that's reverently, slowly, contemplating the Gospel to learn about Jesus.

We feel we know the Gospels by heart. We've been hearing them since we were kids, but the Gospel is always new; the Gospel is always fresh; the Gospel is always daring. The Gospel will always uncover some new insights if we listen with the ears of faith. And our faith tells us that Jesus Christ continues right now, right here, to speak to us, and to teach us, and to heal us, and to challenge us in the words of the Gospel. So a very practical way of just being with Jesus is to take the Gospel and to read it, slowly and reverently, and be with Jesus as He is alive in the Gospel.

There seems to be an explosion of interest in the Word of God in our Church. One of the great spiritual practices that you can develop is simply to take the daily readings from the Liturgy of the Word of the Mass and slowly and reverently meditate on them. That's being with Jesus in the Gospel, letting Him speak to us as He did back then, because He is still alive on the pages of the Gospel.

CONTEMPLATING THE FACE OF CHRIST

A third very practical way we've mentioned before to be with Jesus in prayer is to contemplate the face of Christ. This practice is really old, going back all the way to the early Church Fathers. It died down for awhile but now, this spiritual practice is making a comeback.

As I mentioned in the previous chapter, Pope John Paul II spoke about it very movingly and poetically in *Tertio Millennio Adveniente*, the Pastoral Letter he issued at the close of a great Jubilee Year of 2000, when he invited us to this form of being with Christ in prayer.

In the Transfiguration, Our Lord's face became radiant before St. Peter. His face can still become radiant before us as we contemplate Him in this way.

Some years ago, there was a Synod of Bishops in Rome, out of which came a lot of good interventions. One of them that I thought particularly perceptive came from the future Pope Benedict XVI, Cardinal Joseph Ratzinger. Cardinal Ratzinger said to his brother bishops that he felt the great threat the Church faced today was a chipping away of the reality of Christ. He said we were trying to take away the historical reality of Jesus. And, as usual, Cardinal Ratzinger had a point. As he mentions in his book *Jesus of Nazareth*, the answer to the question "What did Jesus come to do?" is "To give God a face."

Jesus becomes very real to us if we contemplate His face. Our God has a face! Our God is a Person. And when we contemplate the face of the Second Person of the Blessed Trinity, Our Lord and Savior Jesus Christ, in prayer, it is a magnificent way to be with Him.

We picture Him looking hard at us, staring right at us. Sometimes, that chills us. Sometimes, that scares us, because we realize He knows us better than we know ourselves. But we always picture Him looking at us with love, with mercy, and with compassion. Like St. Peter, we want to say, "Lord, it is just good to be with You." We can just be with Christ through prayer, especially prayer before the Eucharist; especially with just reverently reading the Gospel, letting it speak to us, and by contemplating His face.

THE SECOND WAY — SILENCE

A second practical way that we can be with Jesus is through silence. One of the more startling lines in the Gospel in this episode of the Transfiguration is something that you never hear said of St. Peter anywhere else in the Gospels: Peter didn't know what to say.

Peter would have been much better off if that happened more often, if St. Peter wouldn't have said some things that he said in the Gospel. But here we got that line from the Transfiguration where, after Peter says, "Lord, it's good to be here with You," the Gospel elaborates further that "Peter didn't know what to say."

Sometimes, it is a gift when we don't know what to say to Our Lord, because silence is attractive in the eyes of God. There is a divine preference for silence. Silence is essential if we're going to be with Christ. You've got to remember that our contemporary world dreads silence. From the moment we get up with the alarm clock, we want the radio on, the TV on, the telephone ringing, we want messages, we want company, we dread silence. But yet, silence is essential to our life with Christ.

Earlier in this chapter, I mentioned September 11, and the young woman I met on her way into prayer before the Blessed Sacrament. On that same day, I got a call from a priest who was one my seminarians when I was Rector at the North American College in Rome. He said, recounting the day, "Bishop, what a day it has been. Everywhere I turn, people have been asking me things, from the minute we heard about the tragedy."

This priest teaches at a high school. And he said, "I couldn't walk down the hall. The kids were grabbing at me saying, 'Father, explain this. Give us a word. Give us some meaning. Tell us what is going on.'"

Everywhere he went, people were stopping him and saying, "Father, speak to us. Say something!" Then, he told me, "As if that wasn't bad enough, the principal comes and says, 'The radio and TV people are over because they want to interview you, because they say somebody has got to give them a word.' Well, Bishop, I was petrified! I didn't know what to say. I didn't have anything to give them. I was frantic! What was I going to say?

"Finally, I went into the chapel and I closed the door, and I was just quiet. I was just quiet. I let silence reign for five, and then ten, and then twenty minutes — just silence. In that silence I discovered the Word, the Word of God, the Second

Person of the Blessed Trinity. He is the Only Word that I had to give."

You see, this young priest discovered the Word. He discovered what to say in silence. As the body craves silence for sleep, as the mind craves silence for thought, the soul craves silence for prayer, for being with Jesus.

The Church begins every morning by praying, in the Liturgy of the Hours, the *Benedictus* from St. Luke: "In the tender compassion of Our God, the dawn from on high shall come upon us." God's action in our lives is as gentle, tender, subtle, soft, as daily and natural as the quiet of dawn each morning. Dawn is the most still moment of the day, as darkness gives way to light in silence, and it is this traditional stillness that births the new day. It's precisely in such quiet that the Lord comes to us.

"When all things were in quiet silence," the author of the Book of Wisdom says, "and the night was in the midst of her course, thy eternal word leapt down from Heaven from thy royal throne." Christ came to the world in silence. Christ redeemed the world in silence, the silence of the lamb, dumb before its shearer. Christ comes to our hearts now in silence.

BE STILL

Has anybody said it better than the Lord? In the Book of Isaiah we read, "Be still and know that I am God."

I don't know if you've had the chance to read those eloquent words from our Holy Father, Pope Benedict XVI, during his pilgrimage to Poland in 2006, when he visited the death camp at Auschwitz. He just said, "What can one say here? We contemplate the silence of God." It was very profound to have the Vicar of Christ on earth more or less saying, "Where was God in all this?" It is the silence of God.

I was with a group of bishops and rabbis who went to Poland for a Catholic-Jewish dialogue a few years ago, and one of our stops was Auschwitz. I had been to Auschwitz twice before, but never with Jewish people; how well I remember that night. Thet evening, we had a couple of hours of theological reflection, in which we bishops regrettably felt the need to offer a wordy explanation of Auschwitz — the problem of evil, redemptive suffering, what went through our minds when we were there — and we filled up our time with a lot of words. Then the first rabbi who responded, an amazingly insightful and holy man, simply said, "You know, the more I visit Auschwitz, the more I am convinced that the only appropriate response is silence." What a wise, wise man.

I was a graduate priest, only twenty-nine, at the time I took Church history with Msgr. John Tracy Ellis, the great historian, but I've never forgotten what he said.

"You know, the Church would be better off being quiet more often," he would say. "The Church in my day" — which he loved dearly — "always felt obliged to speak on everything and to have all the answers, and always to be making statements. I wonder, the older I get, if the Church would not be better off at times simply remaining silent."

The Church does not have all the answers. She has more — thanks be to God — she has more answers than anyone else because of Divine Revelation, the teaching of the Magisterium, and two thousand years of Sacred Tradition. She has more than anybody else, but she doesn't always have *all* the answers, and sometimes the best answer we can give is silence — reverent, attentive silence.

I like the prayer of C.S. Lewis.

Master, they say when I seem to be in speech with you,
since you make no replies, it's all a dream, one talker aping

two. They are half-right, but not as they imagine; rather, I seek in myself the things I meant to say, and lo! The wells are dry. Then, seeing me empty, you forsake the listener's role and through my dead lips breathe and into utterance wake the thoughts I never knew. And thus, you neither need reply nor can; thus, while we seem two talking, thou art one forever, and I, no dreamer, but thy dream.

This is the power of silence, the power of *being*.

FASTING FROM NOISE

Recently, I was speaking to a rector of perhaps one of the most successful college seminaries going today — St. John Vianney College Seminary, in the Archdiocese of St. Paul and Minneapolis. They have so many college seminarians that they've had to bring trailers in to handle the overflow. The rector was telling me that one night a week the seminarians *fast* from noise. They *fast* from noise.

You know what they do? Get this. And when you think about it, it's very effective from a didactic point of view, in this kind of tactile culture that we live in. The students will bring into the chapel their iPods, their computers, their cell phones, and their television sets. They will literally bring them into the chapel for whatever period of silence they're going to have, fasting from noise. Is it going to be from supper until the next morning? Whenever. They will literally bring them into church and put them there.

The rector told me, "This has been a very prophetic gesture in the house, that the pollution of noise that so infects our young people today, they fast from that." Then he described how, for the first couple months, the first-year men are literally almost in need of Ritalin, because they're just not used to silence. But what an effective spiritual tool it is for them, to get them to fast from noise.

I do try my best to take daily prayer with the utmost seriousness, and the time I most savor is between 4:00 and 5:00 A.M. (I have to be in bed, or at least I try to be in bed, before 11:00 at night). I get some coffee and I head down to chapel — I have a little chapel downstairs. Obviously, I say my Office of readings and Morning Prayer, but then I just try to really remain in some silence, offering up my thoughts and prayers in a quiet morning offering. Then each day I say Mass, usually on the road somewhere, and pray the rest of the Liturgy of the Hours throughout the day, wherever I happen to be. But then at night, when I'm not too good at prayer because I'm exhausted, right before I go to bed I will return to chapel again for just a few moments of silence.

I'm not saying this to brag, because I should be doing ten times more prayer, but at least I'm getting those bookends. My point is, the older I get, as I return to chapel at night and survey the work of the day — and I might have done a lot of things: talked to a lot of movers and shakers, spent some money, transferred some priests, given some talks, or I might have traveled somewhere, or presided at a meeting, or whatever — I'm finding that the older I get, as I survey the day with gratitude, I know it's that time in the morning that was probably most profitable, probably the most valuable time I had all day.

The older I get, I find myself more and more frustrated with all I try to do and accomplish, and I find myself more and more tongue-tied. I'm just wondering what to say to the Lord — I try to tell Him the troubles, I try to tell Him what I'm worried about, the people I promise to pray for, and all. But I'm finding myself more and more saying, "Lord, I'm going to be quiet and

I'm going to be in your presence. You know the prayers that I've promised, and you know the things weighing on my heart and soul, and you know the challenges, and you know the consolations, and I'm just going to be quiet and let you and your heart absorb them, and I'm just going to shut up and quit trying to talk, because you know it anyway. You know the word before I get it on my tongue." I find myself more and more enjoying just being, being with Jesus, sharing company, being silent before Him. I find myself on Mount Tabor with St. Peter, simply saying, "Lord, it's good to be here with You." Because most of the time, I'm so awestruck, like Peter, I hardly know what to say.

Think of the great figures in the Scriptures, like Our Blessed Mother. We don't have many accounts of things she said, do we? She doesn't say much. And her last recorded words in Scripture are simply, "Do whatever He tells you," speaking about Her Son, Our Lord Jesus Christ.

Think about another great figure, St. Joseph. Do you know how many words of St. Joseph we have recorded in the Gospel? Do know how many things we have him saying? Zero! There are no words of St. Joseph recorded in the Gospel. Joseph says nothing in the Scriptures; he truly is a man of silence. And yet, the redemption could not have occurred in the ways we know it without the silence of St. Joseph. He spoke eloquently through his silence.

Think of Our Lord. February is traditionally dedicated to what we call "the hidden life of Jesus." For thirty years, Scripture says nothing about what Jesus might have said or done. He is in silence at Nazareth, preparing for His three years of public life. The Divine Preference is for silence.

Do you never think about one of those familiar episodes of Jesus exorcising a devil in the Gospels? Jesus will be walking along and suddenly He meets someone possessed by the devil. What does Our Lord say? "Be quiet! Shut up! Be still."

Why? Because Our Lord knows that the devil dreads silence. Satan loves clamor. He loves noise and confusion. Because even Satan knows it is in silence, stillness, and quiet that the Word of God comes to us.

"In quiet and confidence shall be thy strength." Have you ever heard of Gerard Manley Hopkins, the famous Jesuit poet? He wrote a poem on silence. I won't recite the whole poem, but just listen to this one statement:

> Elected Silence, sing to me
> And beat upon my whorlèd ear,
> Pipe me to pastures still and be
> The music that I care to hear.

Silence. "Lord, it is good simply to be here with You." St. Peter did not know what to say. Bravo! Sometimes, it's good not to know what to say.

LORD, IT IS GOOD THAT WE ARE HERE WITH YOU

It is good to be with Jesus. To be with Him in prayer, especially before the Eucharist . . . in reverent reading of the Gospel . . . and, especially, contemplating the face of Christ . . . to be with Jesus in silence, not needing to know what to say. In this, as in so many things, St. Peter is a good example.

4.

EMBRACING OUR CROSS

From that time Jesus began to show his disciples that he must go to Jerusalem and suffer many things from the elders and chief priests and scribes, and be killed, and on the third day be raised. And Peter took him and began to rebuke him, saying, "God forbid, Lord! This shall never happen to you." But he turned and said to Peter, "Get behind me, Satan! You are a hindrance to me; for you are not on the side of God, but of men." Then Jesus told his disciples, "If any man would come after me, let him deny himself and take up his cross and follow me."

— Mt. 16:21-24

GET BEHIND ME, SATAN!

You can't help but feel sorry for our friend St. Peter. Even in his moment of acclaim, he blows it trying to talk Our Lord out of the Cross. Remember the context of the sixteenth chapter of St. Matthew's Gospel? He had just professed Jesus Christ as Lord. This is the famous episode when Jesus said to His disciples, "Who do people say that I am?" And it is Peter who says, "You are Christ, the Son of the Living God!"

What a great moment of acclaim and triumph for St. Peter, professing his faith in the divinity of Our Lord. This is the episode where Jesus says, "You are Peter, and on this rock I will build my Church, and I will give you the keys of the Kingdom of Heaven."

It's right after that, when Peter is riding high, that he receives this stern, severe rebuke from Our Lord. Jesus had just told His apostles, after Peter's profession of faith, that He was going to have to go up to Jerusalem, where He would embrace the Cross, suffer, and die. And St. Peter — understandably, I suppose, when you think about it — tries to talk Our Lord out of such a plan. Horrified, he proposes to Jesus that He prevent such a fate. It's this attempt on the part of St. Peter that earns from Our Lord one of the sharpest rebukes we have in the Gospel.

A great Anglican Scripture commentator claimed that, along with the cleansing of the Temple, this is one of two examples of anger on the part of Jesus. I would suggest that we need to look carefully at this episode from the life of Jesus and St. Peter to see why Peter earned such a stern reprimand from Our Lord.

When Peter tried to talk Jesus out of the Cross, Our Lord reacted strongly. For Him and His followers, there's no avoiding the Cross. Satan always tries to talk us out of the Cross. That's why Jesus called Peter "Satan."

St. Augustine, in his magnificent commentary on the sixteenth chapter of St. Matthew's Gospel, wonders if in some way Jesus is not mentally transported back to the forty days He spent fasting in the desert and enduring the temptations of Satan. Remember? At that moment, Satan tried to tempt Jesus out of the Cross. Satan tried to deter Our Lord. Satan wanted to be an obstacle. We recall how Jesus responded to Satan: "Be gone, Satan!" Well, St. Augustine surmised, this is probably what is happening here. It's as if Jesus, closing His eyes and hearing Peter trying to dissuade Him from the Cross, thinks, *Satan's at it again — this time in the form of my friend Peter, the man that I've just made the head of the Church on earth.*

That, of course, earns the rebuke of Jesus. "Get behind me, Satan, for your ways are not God's ways."

We are not startled to find Satan trying to talk Jesus out of the Cross. He's got to, for his own survival, because the Cross is the instrument of his defeat. Satan will always try to talk us, the followers of Jesus, out of the Cross. He will "remonstrate" with us whenever we set out to take up our Cross, because it is the instrument of our victory, the instrument of our salvation. Just as Satan tried to talk Jesus out of the Cross, so he will try to talk us out of the Cross.

The Cross means everything we'd rather not think about: suffering, rejection, adversity, failure, frustration, fatigue, temptation, heartache, doubt, and discouragement. The Cross!

THE NECESSITY OF THE CROSS

If you're going to put out into the deep, the Cross will be there. If you are going to fall in love with Jesus, the Cross will be there. If you're going to let Jesus wash your feet, the Cross will be there. The Cross is the classroom of sanctity, the professor of perfection, the arena of heroic virtue!

"I saw the river over which every soul must pass to reach the Kingdom of God and the name of that river was suffering." So says St. John of the Cross.

The one thing Our Lord can never be accused of is false advertising. How blunt can you get? "Unless you take up your cross and follow Me, you cannot be My disciple." Hardship, sacrifice, suffering, adversity, struggle — it's necessarily going to be part of the life of the disciple.

Not too long ago, I finished a biography on Winston Churchill. I enjoyed what the author wrote about the terribly gloomy, dark time in the history of Great Britain at the beginning of World War II, when Churchill took over from Chamberlain as Prime Minister.

When Sir Winston Churchill was writing his initial speech to the people of England, his handlers tried to talk him out of saying what he had in mind. They said, "Sir Winston, no. This is too bleak. This is too dark. This is too gloomy. This is too pessimistic. We need to be sunny here. We need to be optimistic. You need to be cheerful. You need to be bright."

To which Churchill said, "No. I'm going to say what I just wrote." You probably know the speech: "All I can promise you is blood, sweat, and tears."

The biographer says, in retrospect, that those blunt, realistic words turned the tide; when Dunkirk came, when the bombing of London came, and when near-defeat came, the people remembered those words of Churchill — "All I can promise you is blood, sweat, and tears" — and that realism, that starkness, that honesty, is what galvanized them and kept them going.

Such is Our Leader, my brothers and sisters. Our Lord's handlers, led by our friend St. Peter, tried to talk Him out of it, only to be reprimanded by the Savior. The Cross is a necessary part of discipleship, and Jesus would not be talked out of it.

WHY DOES THE CROSS SURPRISE US?

Our Lord could not be more forthright in telling us that the Cross has to be part of discipleship. Why are we so surprised, then, when it comes?

Not too long ago, I was meeting with a priest who hadn't been ordained very long. He's a great priest; he's worked hard and he's done a great job, but he came in very discouraged, with a whole list of complaints. *The people aren't coming. The people aren't listening. I'm getting criticism. Lot of frustration. Too much work. I'm tired. My pastor really doesn't understand me.* All the usual things.

But I knew he needed to talk, so I let him. Then, I said, "Why are you surprised? Isn't that what was promised to you? Do you not believe that the sacrament of Holy Orders configures you to Jesus Christ, the Head and Shepherd of the Church? And where was Jesus Christ most Head and Shepherd of the Church, if not on the Cross? So why are you startled that you are configured to Christ on the Cross? Why are you shocked that there are setbacks, and frustrations, and temptations, and dryness, and opposition? Why?"

Jesus told us it would come. As a matter of fact, when the Cross comes into your life, I propose that it means you're doing something right. You're on the right track. You're actually following Our Lord, because He told us the Cross would come.

Why, though, are we so slow to learn it? Why, for instance, are we surprised when we find our prayer to be dry, boring, unproductive, and literally have to struggle to persevere sometimes in our prayers? Why are we shocked when we are rejected and mocked for holding true to the values of Christ and His Church? Why are we stunned when people criticize us, lash out at us, blame us, or even hate us? Why are we surprised when temptation and discouragement come, and our fight against sin seems so long and so fatiguing? Why are we surprised when sickness, setback, financial adversity, loneliness, frustration, tension, or stress enters our life? Why are we surprised when fatigue and frustration seem the order of the day? Didn't Jesus tell us that would happen?

All our complaints, all our distresses, are just different words for the Cross. Jesus told us it would come; He invites us to carry that cross with Him to Calvary, thereby to experience His Resurrection.

I love the quote from Thomas à Kempis:

> The cross is always ready. It awaits you everywhere. No matter where you may go, you cannot escape it for wherever you go, you take yourself with you and you shall always find yourself. Turn where you want: above, below, without, or within — you'll find a cross in everything. And everywhere you must have patience, patience if you would have peace within and merit an eternal crown.

The great Lutheran pastor Dietrich Bonhoeffer wrote a magnificent book on this whole topic. He called it *The Cost of Discipleship*. Something tells me that he wasn't surprised when he found himself in front of a Nazi firing squad, because he knew that the cost of discipleship was the Cross.

Why are we so surprised by the presence, the necessity of the Cross in our life? I'll tell you why. Because the world is just like St. Peter and tries to talk us out of the Cross!

What a great teacher Our Lord is. Everything He does means something — even the instrument of His death. It's a sign of contradiction. It's a sign of being diametrically opposed. Something is wrong here. So the Cross is opposed — it's in contradiction — to everything in the world, our culture, our society, and even our unredeemed selves. We don't like the Cross, yet it's there. And so the world will, like St. Peter, constantly try to talk us out of it.

Think about it! You've got a headache, you take an aspirin. You have an unwanted pregnancy, you get rid of it — you abort it. You want sex without responsibility, you wear a condom. Are you inconvenienced by your paralyzed parents? You call a Dr. Kevorkian. Are you struggling in your marriage? You call a lawyer and get divorced. Are you bored being a priest? You take a leave of absence. Is the baby interfering with your career? You drop him off at day care. Are you tired of remaining chaste? You have an affair. Did your doctor tell you to lose weight (mine does)? Well, then, you get another doctor. Are homeless people bothering the posh hotel guest? You hire some security guards to herd them away. Are you caught with the results of a mistake? You lie and you wiggle your way out of it.

Doesn't it all boil down to St. Peter's well-intentioned intervention, "Lord, no more of this talk about going to Jerusalem to suffer and die. No more of this chatter about the Cross. Forget all that stuff"?

Satan unrelentingly tries to convince us that the Cross can and should be avoided; that it is an anomaly; that it is a sign of failure; that it means we're doing something wrong. But Jesus tells us, "No! The cross is a sign of victory, obedience, love, selflessness, total dependence upon God. It is the road to salvation. It is a sign of complete union with Me." It's actually a vindication that you're doing something *right*.

THE PRESENT CROSS

I don't believe there's ever been an era in the Church when the Body of Christ, the Church, has been free from the Cross. It can't be. I just mentioned that it's an essential, inescapable part of our following Christ. That's been true all the time. But I don't think I'd be guilty of hyperbole to say that the Cross is particularly evident for us right now, and the Cross that priests bear is a particularly heavy share of the Cross.

Bishops and priests seem to be catching it from all sides. It seems that every move, every word, every decision is scrutinized and misinterpreted by some segment in our polarized Church. The far right detests us because they say we're all modernists and homosexuals. The far left despises us because we're all into a patriarchal, oppressive, conservative, homophobic Church. Not too long ago, at the beginning of Lent, I found myself at Night Prayer succumbing to a whine, a lament, and saying, "Lord, what am I doing wrong? Why doesn't anybody like me anymore? Why am I afraid to read the paper in the morning? Why am I afraid to open my e-mail? Why am I afraid to open a letter that comes in marked 'personal and confidential'? Why am I afraid to answer the phone? Why am I afraid to greet people anymore, not knowing what they're going to say or what they're going to ask? Why do I dread sometimes just the work of the day? What am I doing wrong, Lord?"

Then I raised my head from this whining lament of self-pity and caught sight of the crucifix that hangs in the little chapel in the basement. It was the first crucifix I can ever remember as a child, made by the founding pastor of my home parish — who was a carpenter — and it hung upon the altar in our temporary church when I was a kid. The parish gave it to me when I came up to Milwaukee, so it's there. It has a special place in my heart. And as I looked at Jesus there on the Cross, I could almost — in the spirit of contemplation, according to St. Ignatius of Loyola — I could almost picture Our Lord smiling at me and saying to me, "Get behind me, Satan. Why are you trying to talk Me, and yourself, out of the Cross?" When opposition and misunderstanding come, as long as they come for doing the right thing, we rejoice. We're closer to Jesus.

I remember the spiritual director I had when I was newly ordained saying, "You'll know you are getting old when you start to like the Psalms." Well, I must be getting there, because the Psalms make more and more sense to me — especially those where the Psalmist is feeling beat up, or is "letting off steam" with the Lord.

I am moved to think these were the prayers of Jesus, who would have known the Psalms by heart. He repeated them, as we know from his quote of Psalm 22on the Cross: "My God, my God, why have your forsaken me?"

The Psalms have come to be so much for me. They are like an opening chapter to the Passion of Our Lord. Do we believe with all our heart and soul that by the Sacrament of Baptism we've been united with God, we've been united with Jesus, we've been transformed and recreated in His own image and likeness, after the pattern of His only-begotten Son? So it's no surprise to find ourselves there on the Cross with Our Lord.

SHOW ME YOUR WOUNDS

When I was rector at the North American College in Rome, I was present at the beatification of Padre Pio, who is very popular in Italy. He's up with St. Francis as probably the most popular of saints. In fact, when my little niece, Shannon, had cancer, the Italian workers at the North American College would always ask me how she was doing.

One day, Vitorio, one of the workers, said, "How is Shannon, Monsignor?"

I said, "She's really sick, Vitorio. Would you please pray to Jesus for her?"

"No, I don't pray to Jesus," he answered. "I go right to Padre Pio."

I think he flunked his Christology course, but that's how popular Padre Pio is there.

At Padre Pio's beatification, tons of Americans came, and a lot of them came to the North American College for a reception. It was there that I met a number of men who had visited with Padre Pio at San Giovanni Rotondo after World War II.

"We went to see Padre Pio," one of the veterans said, "And I was as skeptical as can be. The other guys, they thought this was great. But I thought, 'I'll go along. Maybe we'll meet some nice-looking Italian girls down in southern Italy, because I don't believe in this fraud.'"

As it turned out, they were able to go to Padre Pio's early Mass, and afterward, they were able to meet him. When Padre Pio came to greet this guy, the American demanded, "Show me your wounds." Because the Vatican had ordered Padre Pio to cover his stigmata — they didn't want people capitalizing on them — the wounds were covered with gloves. So the guy said to Padre Pio, "Show me your wounds. I don't believe you."

Padre Pio looked at him and said, "Show me yours."

"I don't claim to have the stigmata. You do. Show me your wounds," the veteran repeated.

Padre Pio only said again, "Show me yours."

"What are you talking about?" The guy was an Italian American. He knew Italian, so he knew he was hearing Padre Pio right. He just didn't understand. So Padre Pio explained:

"Well, we've all got wounds. We all bear the stigmata. We've all got the wounds of the Cross. Mine, for some strange reason, happen to be visible, but so what? You've got them, too. You're carrying some. I can see them."

With that, the guy said, he began to weep, and Padre Pio said, "Come with me." They went into the confessional, where Padre Pio invited him one more time, "Show me your wounds."

The guy then admitted that, at that moment, he was bearing a tremendous cross. At Anzio, he had landed with his two buddies — the three of them together — and his two buddies were wounded. They were pinned down by machine guns. But he went ahead and left them behind, even as they yelled after him, "Please come get us." But he didn't. He left, he escaped; and he said this was a horror, a nightmare, a devil — a wound that he had borne for a long time, one he was finally able to reveal to that holy man.

"Show me your wounds." We've all got them. We've all got the stigmata. We all have a share in the Cross of Christ. The world still taunts us with Him — "Come down off that cross and show us you're really God"— like they did on Calvary that first Good Friday, and yet we cling to the Cross because that's where our God is, and that's where His divinity is most obvious.

FACING THE CROSS

Satan tries to convince us that the Cross a sign of failure; Our Lord Jesus Christ tells us it's a sign of victory. Facing and embracing our Cross is the way to our salvation — and that's why Satan hates it! That's why he tries to talk us out of it, because he doesn't want us to reach salvation.

The world doesn't want a Church on the Cross, either. We want a Church to be fashioned to our own convenient, comfortable ideas:

"We'll believe if you will come down off the Cross and quit talking about all this sexual morality and condemning abortion."

"We will believe if you will allow women priests."

"I'll be a priest if you'll let me get married."

"I'll come back to the Church if you'll approve my second marriage."

"I'll believe if you'll keep quiet about civil rights."

"I'll join if you'll shut up about our duty and social justice to the poor."

Isn't all of this just another version of the taunts of those at the foot of the Cross on that first Good Friday? "Come down off the cross, and then we'll believe!"

"No more talking about this suffering," taunts St. Peter. And Jesus says, "I will show you that I am God by being here on the Cross." Because nowhere was the divinity and the power of Jesus Christ, the only-begotten Son of God, more evident than when He was on the Cross. Nowhere was He more helpless, but nowhere did He accomplish more — the salvation of the world and opening the gates of Heaven — than on the Cross.

Instead, what we seem to want to believe is that "A God without wrath brought men without sin into a kingdom without judgment through a Christ without a cross," as Richard Nieber critiques so much of our contemporary thought.

My first pastor back home in St. Louis — I mention him a lot — whenever he would have the marriage of a young couple, he would present them with a crucifix.

"Look, I'm giving you this crucifix for two reasons," he would say. "First of all, you're starting a new home, and no Catholic home should be without crucifix.

"The second reason I'm giving you a crucifix, here at your wedding ceremony, is because I want you to put it in the house and, every time you look at the Cross, be reminded that if your married love is to be pure, faithful, and fruitful, it will have to have a share in the Cross. The struggle and the suffering of the Cross will be part of your marriage. And when the Cross comes — when those setbacks, those frustrations, those arguments, and those tensions come — don't you ask what is wrong with your marriage. You thank God there's something *right* with your marriage, because your marriage is sharing in the Cross."

THE WAYS WE EXPERIENCE THE CROSS

If we wish to grow in our intimacy with Jesus, we must be willing not only to live for Him, but to die with Him. The Cross will be a part of our life, and we can't be surprised when it comes. In our Christian life, it seems to me, the Cross can come to us in three ways.

First of all, the Cross comes to everybody, whether they are disciples of Christ or not. Everyone experiences the Cross in the simple, ordinary adversities of life. Getting up in the morning can be part of the Cross, right? That share in the Cross doesn't just come to disciples of Jesus. But that's one way the Cross can come to us, because we live in an imperfect creation where there's always going to be tension, where there's always going to be struggle and adversity.

A second way the Cross enters our life is when we suffer because of our loyalty to Christ, His Church, and the Gospel. I'm thinking of a young woman that I met a couple years ago who made a lot of financial sacrifices to get through nursing school and was hired by one of the premier medical facilities in this country. Then, on her second day on the job, she was asked to participate in an abortion. She wouldn't do it, and they fired her. That woman knows the cost of discipleship. She is sharing in the Cross, losing her job — losing something she worked long and hard for — because of her allegiance to Christ and His Gospel.

A third way we share in the Cross is through taking upon ourselves voluntary acts of penance and mortification, trying to conform ourselves to the suffering of Jesus on the Cross. That, of course, is a very common and most laudable thing to do all the time, but especially during the season of Lent. However we do it, whenever we do it, the Cross has got to be part of our life.

When I was in Rome, I was blessed to have the presence of a very faithful priest of the Diocese of Scranton. This priest, who is like a brother to me, is one of the most selfless, generous priests that I know. About twenty years ago, he was diagnosed with multiple sclerosis. While he served as vice-rector, we could see the ravages of this disease catch up with him. The entire community loved him very much and rallied around him. As we watched him bear his Cross, it became a cross for all of us as well, because we were in such solidarity with him.

I remember one day at Mass, he came down from the chair and was going over to the pulpit to preach when his legs buckled on him. He would have fallen down, except he was close enough to the altar that he grabbed onto it very quickly. Then, he regained his balance, straightened up, and looked at all of us.

"I better give my sermon holding onto the altar," he said, "or I'm going to fall." Then, after a pause, he went on, "And maybe that's a good enough homily for today."

The power of that! That man, bearing his cross, holding onto the altar for dear life — that altar which for us represents the Cross, the altar of sacrifice, where Calvary is renewed at every Mass . . . that brave, generous priest, saying, "If I don't hold onto this altar, if I don't embrace this cross , I'm really going to stumble and fall" . . . was one of the best homilies I've ever heard. And two of the seminarians said afterward that it was at that moment when they reaffirmed their priestly vocation.

KEEP YOUR EYE FOCUSED ON CHRIST

At one of the parishes where I was assigned in St. Louis, I especially loved going on my Communion calls. I had the privilege of bringing Holy Communion every Friday to a great man by the name of Charles. I didn't know him when he was still young; when I encountered him, he was in his mid-to-late fifties and completely paralyzed by a stroke. The other people in the parish used to recount that prior to that incident, he'd been a strapping, handsome, athletic man.

I used to go to his house, and there he would be on a hospital bed in the living room, with his wife nearby, who was so loving and tender. We couldn't converse, but when his wife would come, Charles could blink his eyes and she would interpret what he meant. That was how they would communicate. I'd ask Charles a question, and then he'd blink, and his wife would translate for me. Through it all, he always seemed to be serene, and at peace.

Well, one day I was visiting as usual, standing there talking to him, when his wife said, "Oh excuse me for a minute, Father. I've got to go into the kitchen for something." But suddenly, when she left, I could detect Charlie becoming uncharacteristically agitated. He was blinking furiously, and I could see that his usual tranquility and peace wasn't there. This was so frustrating, because I knew something was wrong but couldn't find out what it was. Finally, after what seemed like an eternity, his wife came back in, and I said, "Help me, Margaret. Something is wrong with Charlie. He's bothered, and he's agitated."

With a glance at where I was standing, she just smiled. "Oh, yeah, move over a little. You're blocking the Cross."

I looked behind me, and there in his direct line of sight — where Charles would always stare, right in front of him, because he couldn't turn his head — was the crucifix. And it dawned on me then what was going on. This man had his eyes locked on Jesus on the Cross, and that was what gave him meaning and purpose to his life. That's why he could have that sense of serenity and peace, because he was carrying his cross with Christ.

I learned a lesson there. I learned a lesson that St. Peter learned as well: never, ever block the Cross.

5.

How Do We Let God Love Us?

Now before the feast of the Passover, when Jesus knew that his hour had come to depart out of this world to the Father, having loved his own who were in the world, he loved them to the end. And during supper, when the devil had already put it into the heart of Judas Iscariot, Simon's son, to betray him, Jesus, knowing that the Father had given all things into his hands, and that he had come from God and was going to God, rose from supper, laid aside his garments, and girded himself with a towel. Then he poured water into a basin, and began to wash the disciples' feet, and to wipe them with the towel with which he was girded. He came to Simon Peter; and Peter said to him, "Lord, do you wash my feet?" Jesus answered him, "What I am doing you do not know now, but afterward you will understand." Peter said to him, "You shall never wash my feet." Jesus answered him, "If I do not wash you, you have no part in me." Simon Peter said to him, "Lord, not my feet only but also my hands and my head!" Jesus said to him, "He who has bathed does not need to wash, except for his feet, but he is clean all over; and you are clean, but not every one of you." For he knew who was to betray him; that was why he said, "You are not all clean."

When he had washed their feet, and taken his garments, and resumed his place, he said to them, "Do you know what I have done to you? You call me Teacher and

Lord; and you are right, for so I am. If I then, your Lord
and Teacher, have washed your feet, you also ought to
wash one another's feet. For I have given you an example, that you also should do as I have done to you."

— Jn. 13:1-15

I Have Given You an Example

"Lord, wash not only my feet but also my hands and my
head!" This selection from John's Gospel obviously transports
us back to Holy Thursday. We're all very familiar with this
passage, the washing of the feet. And when we contemplate
this scene from the Gospel, we usually interpret it as a very
dramatic sign from Our Lord of selfless service to His disciples on the day before His Passion. He is giving them one
final example of caring for one another, of loving one another,
of ministering to one another, of serving one another. Then,
He tells them to go do the same: the *Mandatum* (meaning
commandment, after the new commandment He gave them),
to go care for one another and to love one another in the same
way as He has just done, by washing their feet. So, most of the
time, do we not interpret this beautiful, moving, dramatic sign
of Jesus taking upon himself the condition of the slave, and
serving His brothers by washing their feet, as a dramatic sign
and call from Christ for us to serve other people?

That's a very correct interpretation, and I'm not going to
try to contradict that or downplay that in this chapter. But
what I would propose is that in this passage, Jesus is also telling
us something else. He's not only giving us an example and
mandating that we follow that example in serving others, in
washing the feet of others. He is also telling us that He wants
to wash *our* feet.

Jesus wants to minister to us in a very basic way. He wants to care for us. He wants to love us. He wants to tend to us. He wants to soothe and console us. And I would propose to you — and I don't think you would contradict me — that when faced with that, we find ourselves very much like St. Peter. It's hard for us to let Jesus serve us. It's difficult for us to allow the Master to wash our feet.

I don't know why that's so. We're sort of reluctant to be put in the position of having Jesus wait on us, to serve us, or to care for us. We're uncomfortable with the thought of Jesus washing our feet. He is Our Lord and Master, and aren't we called to wash the feet of others? That, we're all right with, even if we try to avoid it on occasion — we're very much at peace with that *Mandatum*, that order, that encouragement, to wash the feet of others. But I find that often I'm like St. Peter, reluctant to allow Jesus to wash my feet. In this chapter, then, I'd exhort you to let Jesus wash your feet.

God Is Love

I've been very moved by the writings of the Benedictine Abbot Blessed Columba Marmion. I find him very profound. Abbot Marmion tells us that every sacrament we celebrate returns us to the day of our baptism. He says that on the day of our baptism, as helpless babies, we were carried by someone else to be washed clean in the saving waters of that font and receive that powerful first sacrament. This was the first time that Jesus "washed our feet." He wants to continue to do that, if we will only let Him. Jesus *wants* to serve us, to minister to us. He literally wants to wash our feet.

Yet I admit that I find letting Him do this is tougher than me washing the feet of other people. Why? I don't know if it's my pride or my sense of independence. I don't know if it's my manliness, my identity as a priest and bishop. I think we're used to being the ones who are supposed to be doing the serving, the ministering, the washing, not receiving it. So I find myself a bit resistant to the Lord's desire to wash my feet. It all comes down to a simple, yet profound, fact: I would maintain that the most effective way we allow the Master to wash our feet is by humbly and gratefully accepting His passionate love for us.

In the thirteenth chapter of St. John's Gospel, the opening line reads:

> Now before the feast of the Passover, when Jesus knew that his hour had come to depart out of this world to the Father, having loved his own who were in the world, he loved them to the end.

This is Jesus loving His disciples. St. John says elsewhere, "In this is love, not that we loved God but that he loved us" (1 Jn. 4:10). One of the great leaps that we make in our growth as followers of Our Lord is admitting the absolute primacy of the fact that God loves us first. To gratefully and humbly accept that love, totally undeserved, is a beautiful way to allow Him to wash our feet.

You've probably heard the story of St. John, the last of the twelve apostles to die. Tradition tells us that he didn't die a martyr's death, but lived on the Isle of Patmos to a very advanced age. Toward the end of St. John's life, hundreds and hundreds of people would make the journey to the Isle of Patmos to be with him for the Sunday Eucharist. Every Sunday, his disciples would carry St. John down from the cave where he was living to be with the people, and every Sunday, John the Evangelist would say the same thing:

"Little children, God loves you. Love Him and love one another. Little children, God loves you; now, you love Him and love one another."

He would say it over and over and over again; people there to hear his teaching would hear that same thing repeatedly:

"Little children, God loves you, and He wants you to love Him and love one another."

Finally, somebody said, "Father, why do you keep saying that over and over again?"

And John answered, "Because the Master kept saying it over and over again."

That's what it's all about: the primacy of God's love for us.

GOD'S LOVE FOR US

In my first assignment, very often the pastor and I would take a walk after supper, and we would be joined by a very prominent Jewish psychiatrist from St. Louis. We enjoyed his company and conversation very much, but I especially remember one night in particular. That night, he said to us, "You know, if I understand something about your religion as Christians, you could put me out of business."

We chuckled. But then, the pastor asked, "What are you talking about?"

The psychiatrist said, "Well, if I understand the Christian faith correctly, your major tenet is that God loves you passionately, individually, by name, and that this love is the core of the universe, the source of all meaning. I have discovered that almost every emotional struggle that people go through and see me about — almost every psychosis or neurosis — boils down to the fact that that person thinks he or she is not worthy of anybody's love. He or she doesn't love himself or herself. So if this message, this good news of Christianity, ever sinks in that you are passionately, individually loved by God, I'm out of business."

I'll never forget that. This man had caught the message of the Gospel: that God, through His Son, Jesus, has revealed the passionate, personal love that God has for each one of us in creation.

So, before we can love His people or even love God back, we must gratefully and humbly accept His love. We must allow Jesus to love us. We must allow Jesus to wash our feet as an act of love.

If you've gone through St. Ignatius Loyola's spiritual exercises, you will remember that one of the pivotal moments right off the bat is that we have a grasp of our sinfulness, our nothingness, our unworthiness — quickly followed by a humble, grateful acceptance of God's passionate love for us. We don't deserve it. We haven't earned it. We can't achieve it. We can't win it. But we simply open up ourselves with gratitude and humility, conscious of our nothingness, our unworthiness, our darkness, and allow God to tenderly love us.

St. Alphonsus Ligouri wrote:

> From all eternity God has loved us, and it is in this vein that he speaks to us. "Oh, man, consider carefully that I first loved you. You had not even appeared in the light of day, nor did the world itself even exist, but already I loved you. From all eternity I have loved you."

There it is again: the primacy of God's overwhelmingly passionate, tender love for us.

Allowing God to Fill the Reservoir
The beginning of all sanctity, the starting point for all discipleship, then, is not us loving God or loving His people; it's us

humbly, gratefully accepting God's passionate love for us. We savor it, we bask in it, and then — only then — can we return it to God and to His people.

I say this of myself as much as I propose it to you. I am afraid we usually start backwards. We usually say, "Okay, God, wait a minute. Let me show You how much I love you:

"Let me do all these things for You.

"Let me say all these prayers.

"Let me accomplish all these virtues and good works.

"Let me love Your people to death.

"Let me do all that, Lord, and then, then, then, maybe, maybe, *maybe* I'll earn Your love, and maybe I can win Your love, and maybe I can just achieve acceptance and salvation."

At that — figuratively speaking, of course — God is beating His head against the wall and saying:

"You've got it backwards. First, accept My love for you.

"You can't earn it.

"You can't win it.

"You can't achieve it.

"You can't merit it.

"Just accept it gratefully and humbly, and then give it back to Me; then give it to My people."

We say, "No! You're not going to wash my feet. Oh, no. I'm going to go out and wash others', that's fine. I might even wash Yours, Lord, but You're not going to wash my feet."

But, like Jesus, God just says, "Sit back and relax and let me wash your feet, because if I do not wash you, you have no part in Me." Only at that point, with Peter, do we finally say, "Lord, not my feet only but also my hands and my head!"

How blessed we are, because it's different with human relationships, is it not? When we talk about the love between a man and a woman, or when we talk about a friendship with anybody else, much of the time we've got to prove our love to them and earn our love from them. That's very true in human relationships. But it's not true in the primary relationship — our relationship with God. His love is a given. It seems too good to be true, but we've got to believe it, because it's the beginning of all sanctity — to humbly, gratefully accept God's overwhelmingly personal love for us, and then to return it to Him and to His people.

St. Bernard of Clairvaux, that great mystic, erudite theologian, and renowned preacher, says this beautifully: "Before you can be a channel, you have got to be a reservoir."

Think about what St. Bernard is saying. Most of us are pretty good at being channels, are we not? Throughout your life, you've been a darned good channel. You've channeled the Lord's mercy to your children. You've channeled His grace, His compassion, His word, and His goodness to those you've dealt with in your life. Most of us are pretty good channels. But we're not too good at being reservoirs; only what St. Bernard says is that if we don't have a reservoir within, where we are filled within with those life-giving waters of God's love, mercy, compassion, and salvation — well, then, the channel is going to dry up, and there is not going to be anything we can bring to His people.

First, be a reservoir. Then, be a channel. It's almost as if St. Bernard's saying first, let Jesus wash *your* feet, and then you can wash others'. First, allow Our Lord to minister to *you*, and then you can minister to other people. That's a tough lesson to learn.

Receptive of God's Love
Bishop Robert Morneau, the auxiliary bishop in Green Bay, Wisconsin, states it well. He writes, "The principle that God

first loves us places us in the position of being a respondent, rather than an initiator, in the adventure called the spiritual life."

I sometimes think that the female saints have an easier time understanding this. I'm thinking of Catherine of Siena, Edith Stein, Faustina, Gertrude, and Bridget of Sweden. If you read their writings, you see that they seem to be wonderfully aware of God loving them first, and they seem to have no difficulty being recipients of that love. They are comfortable being a recipient rather than an initiator, receiving God's overwhelmingly tender, passionate, personal love for them. Not only do they accept it — they bask in it, they cherish it, they savor it, and then, they return it. They seem to have less trouble than most of us in allowing Jesus to wash their feet.

Remember that earth-shattering insight of St. Thérèse of the Child Jesus, the Little Flower, when she was so desperate to discover her vocation in the Church? She dreamed about being a missionary in China, or going into the prisons to win souls for Jesus. But none of these was her vocation. Rather, one day she simply discovered that her vocation was to accept God's love and to return it to Him, to be loved by God and to give it back.

Ever since the election of our Holy Father, Pope Benedict XVI, in April of 2005, everyone was trying to figure out what his first encyclical would be about. Remember? A pope's first encyclical is often thought to be almost an "inaugural address" of a new pontificate. There were these great speculations: He's going to speak about medical moral issues; he's going to speak about the conversion of Europe; he's going to speak about Islam; he's going to speak about the danger of moral relativism; and on and on. So what did he write on? *Deus caritas est*, "God is love." That's so darned simple, it's profound. He returns to the basic Christian revelation that God loves us passionately, tenderly, personally, and then asks us to return that love back to Him and His people.

How do we let God love us? Are there some practical, everyday ways that we can just allow ourselves to be loved by God, and accept that love, before ever even thinking about the duty that we have to return it to Him and other people? I think there are. None of them will surprise you.

Receptive Prayer

The first practical way, I would submit, would be prayer. I'm talking about a specific form of prayer. For me — and I'm guessing this may be true of you — most of the time when I speak of prayer, I mean doing something for God: I pray my Divine Office; I celebrate the Eucharist; I spend some time at the Rosary and devotions. I love those, and they need to be a constant element of my spiritual regimen. These are all an active form of prayer, are they not? This sort of prayer has us giving God praise, glory, and honor, as well as expressing our contrition and our needs to Him. All excellent forms of prayer, and we need them desperately.

Unfortunately, that's about 99 percent of my prayer. There should always be a balance with what one might call a more passive kind of prayer. This has been a struggle for me since the days in the seminary: approaching prayer as simply basking, — usually silently — and receiving, letting God's love immerse me in grace. That, of course, is allowing Jesus to wash our feet. That is simply sitting back humbly and gratefully and accepting God's love. That's a tough kind of prayer. If we master that one, well, then, we're on the way to sanctity, and that's the one that is evasive. I try my best, you see, and it's tough. I'll take my breviary, I'll take my rosary, I'll take my book of devotions, I'll take my spiritual reading, but then comes that time when I just want to sit back and allow God's love to sink in, to accept His love — that's the tough one.

I find myself distracted. I find myself itching to do something. It's almost as if I'm saying to the Lord, "Oh, You're not going to wash my feet." When that happens, do you know what I do? I literally picture Jesus saying to me, "Timothy, if I don't wash your feet, you can't have anything to do with Me," and it's then I will say, "Well then, Lord, wash not only my feet but my head and my hands, as well."

If I take this a step further, it gets interesting:

"Lord, wash my head. It's filled with distractions. It's filled with anxiety.

"Wash my eyes. I don't like what I see.

"Wash my mouth. I eat too much.

"Wash my throat. I don't speak well all the time.

"Wash my heart. It's filled with love that shouldn't be there.

"Wash my belly. I make it a god."

"Lord, go ahead. Wash, wash every section of my body. Let me just bask in your love."

Have any of you men ever been shaved by a barber? That used to be common. In Italy, still they do it a lot. On some Thursdays, when we had a day off from school, I would go to get a haircut, and I'd always get a shave as well. That is one of the greatest pleasures you can have, to allow someone to shave you — but it's uncomfortable at first. You sit in a chair and have somebody lather up your face, sharpen a knife and put it to your neck, and start to shave you. That was uncomfortable, to allow somebody to get that close, to be so vulnerable to let somebody do that elementary service, one I'm so used to doing by myself every morning of my life. But once I allowed that barber to do it, it became a great pleasure that I looked forward to.

Such as it is when we do this kind of passive prayer. We're allowing Our Lord to shave us, to wash our feet. *Let me take care of you. Timothy, let me tell you that I love you. Believe me. Put your head on my shoulder. Listen to me. Let me comfort you. Let me console you.* That's the passive kind of prayer that I suggest that we very much need.

RECEIVING THE EUCHARIST

The second way that we can allow Jesus to wash our feet is through the Eucharist. We are apt to think of our celebration of Eucharist as a duty, something that we have to do for God, and rightly so. It is the greatest thing that any of us can do, the greatest way that we can, in union with Christ on Calvary, offer our Heavenly Father praise, satisfaction, atonement, contrition, intercession, and thanksgiving. It is the greatest act we can do for God and His people, no doubt about it.

But the temptation is for us to look at the Holy Eucharist only as us doing something for God, which is only half the story. The Eucharist is also primarily us allowing God to do something *for* us and His people.

It is us opening up — there we go again, opening up — in vulnerability, humility, and gratitude, simply allowing God to do something for us, to fill our hearts and souls with His grace, to feed our souls with the very Body and Blood of His only-begotten Son, who is really and truly there, Body, Blood, Soul, and Divinity.

Think about this the next time you approach to receive the Eucharist. God is offering you His love, so the Eucharist can become, again, that way that we allow Jesus daily to wash our feet.

ALLOWING GOD TO FORGIVE US

A third way that I find very practical — when I sense that I am saying, "Lord, I'm going to let you wash my feet" — would be whenever I celebrate the sacrament of Reconciliation (Penance). Once again, when I prepare for the sacrament of Penance, I usually think, *This is a spiritual duty, a high duty that I have as a disciple, as a Christian, as a Catholic, as a priest, to frequently approach this tribunal of mercy. This is a requirement of my spiritual life.* It is all of this, but it's also, once again, allowing Jesus to love us, to forgive us.

Padre Pio says very beautifully that we approach the sacrament of Penance often not because we realize that we have not loved God, but because we realize we love Him so much that we don't want to hurt Him. So it's an act of love and an act of allowing God to love us. It's an act of allowing God to hold us, embrace us, forgive us, and extend His mercy to us.

We must be careful to avoid a Pelagian approach: the notion that the sacraments are something that we do for God, rather than a free gift offered to us from God. I get beautiful letters from our young people, asking for the sacrament of Confirmation, for instance Most of them are moving, but there's always a tenor there such as:

"Dear Archbishop Dolan, I really deserve this sacrament because I've done all that is required, and now I want it," or "I'm approaching this sacrament, this is going to be my time to stand up and say to God, 'Boy, God, you need me. I am really a great person, and I'm going to do you a big favor and commit myself to your Church.'"

Of course, that's a totally un-Catholic way of appreciating the sacraments. That's Pelagianism, isn't it, a belief we *earn* God's grace? The essence of the sacrament of Confirmation, the essence of the Eucharist, the essence of Penance, is that a sacrament simply asks us to open up, in humility and gratitude, to let God work salvation within us. He does that for us in a very personal way in the sacrament of Penance. I think of Him in the sacrament of Penance as washing my feet.

Fr. Mark O'Keefe, O.S.B., the former rector of St. Meinrad Seminary, writes:

> Conversion, which comes from the Sacrament of Penance . . . is a response to the outpouring of God's love and the grateful acceptance of the friendship that God offers to us as sinners.

Well, do we believe it or not? Abbott Marmion says:

> If every sacrament is a return to our baptism, then in every prayer, every sacrament we're a baby and we're being held in the arms of Holy Mother Church, and we are helpless, and there is nothing we can do but cry. We can't earn anything, we can't deserve anything, we are totally vulnerable and helpless, and we are simply open in humility and gratitude to the love that God wants to give us.

God loves us first. And, like St. Peter, we don't like that. We want to say, "Let me love You, Lord . . . then maybe, maybe, *maybe* I'll accept Yours." And Jesus says, "Peter, if I don't wash your feet, you can't have anything to do with Me." To that, we can only say, "Then Lord, I accept your love. I bask in it. And Lord, wash not only my feet but my head and my hands, as well."

6.

DO YOU LOVE THE LORD?

When they had finished breakfast, Jesus said to Simon Peter, "Simon, son of John, do you love me more than these?" He said to him, "Yes, Lord; you know that I love you." He said to him, "Feed my lambs." A second time he said to him, "Simon, son of John, do you love me?" He said to him, "Yes, Lord; you know that I love you." He said to him, "Tend my sheep." He said to him the third time, "Simon, son of John, do you love me?" Peter was grieved because he said to him the third time, "Do you love me?" And he said to him, "Lord, you know everything; you know that I love you." Jesus said to him, "Feed my sheep."

— Jn. 21:15-17

"GOD WANTS US TO LOVE HIM BACK"

One of my favorite quotes from Pope John Paul the Great was something that he said to priests: "Love for Jesus and His Church is the passion of your lives."

Once when I was a parish priest, teaching the fourth-grade class in the parish school about the life of Our Lord, I asked the fourth-graders if they could define for me what exactly the "Good News" was. We use that phrase so often, "the Good News." I said to the fourth-graders, "What is the Good News?" I'll never forget what one fourth-grade girl said to me in answer to my question: "Father, the Good News is that God loves us a lot, and He wants us to love Him back."

That's not a bad definition of the Good News, is it?

The essence of Christianity — the essence of our life with God — is a love relationship with the Lord. What Jesus asks St. Peter in the Gospel passage at the beginning of this chapter, He also asks us: "Do you love Me?"

We picture ourselves in the Gospel passage, and imagine Jesus saying to us, "Timothy, do you love me?" "Sarah, do you love me?" "Charlie, do you love me?" And we answer, "Lord, you know everything. Yes, Lord, we love You."

That having been said, we'd all like to love Him a lot more. I don't think any of us is all that happy and content with our love relationship with Jesus; at least I hope we are not. Because we should all want to intensify that love relationship with Our Lord.

Some good questions to ask ourselves . . .

How can I love Our Lord more deeply?

How can I love Our Lord more fervently?

How can I respond with all the enthusiasm in my heart, like St. Peter did when Jesus said to him, "Peter, do you love Me?"

How can I respond with excitement and fervor, "Yes, Lord, I do love You"?

Or if, sadly — and these things do happen — if we admit in all candor that, as a matter of fact, we have fallen out of love with Him, and if our love for the Master has become cold or lifeless, how can we rekindle that? How can we re-fall in love with Our Lord?

How Can I Love Our Lord More?

I'm going to propose to you a little strategy here. We will deepen our love relationship with Our Lord — which is the essence of the spiritual life — in the same way that a man and woman fall in love or deepen their relationship with each other.

Archbishop Fulton Sheen used to say that one of the ways of talking about our relationship with the Lord is to think of the relationship of love on a human scale. So our relationship with the Lord is very analogous to the relationship of a husband and wife, or an engaged couple, or a couple falling in love, or a friendship that we would have with a man or a woman that is very sustaining, pure, and chaste, but a very beautiful, loving friendship. So you'll see some of the same aspects to these very human relationships that we can have in a relationship with the Lord.

In other words, we can look for an analogy to the way a man and a woman begin to date, to court, to fall in love, prepare for marriage, and then spend their married life trying to intensify their married love.

Recently, I've been able to watch my brother Patrick fall in love with Mary Theresa Kelly and get married, and I've seen certain characteristics. So let's talk about nine very simple ways that we can intensify our love for Jesus, or rekindle our love for Jesus if it has gotten tepid.

Spending Time with Our Lord

The first thing we do whenever we fall in love with someone, or want to intensify our love with that person, is spend time with them. Not long ago, I reviewed an excellent series that the Archdiocese of St. Louis is putting out for Christian marriage. One of the points that they emphasize for young couples preparing for marriage is that you must give one another the gift of time. If you don't spend quality time together every day, your love is going to go flat.

Do we spend time with Our Lord? You know time is one of the most precious gifts we have to give. I have heard many retired people say that they looked forward to retirement because they thought they would have a lot more time to read, pray, and grow in their relationship with the Lord — only to find themselves and their lives still filled with distractions and difficulties so much that they're still not able to do it. Time is a precious gift that we have to give.

When I was a parish priest working with couples to prepare them for marriage, I would always find that the questions that would cause arguments were questions about time, because usually the woman would expect a lot more time from the man than he was prepared to give. And, as you know, many of the arguments in marriages, many of the arguments in friendships, are about time. "You don't give me as much time as I think I deserve. Our friendship, our relationship takes a lot of time. And are we willing to give that?"

When I pray, sometimes I find I look more often at my watch than I do at the crucifix or the tabernacle. One of the most difficult frenzies I've ever been in was losing my calendar. This was before I was a bishop; now, I don't have one, because everybody else tells me where I'm supposed to be. But when I was a priest, I lost my calendar, and *I* was lost! Because of how every hour and every day was scheduled, if I didn't have this book, I didn't know where I was supposed to go. It reminded me of what a prisoner I was of time — the calendar and the clock.

We have to spend time with Our Lord. And the only way we spend time with Him — here I go again — is through prayer. I keep coming back to this. No human love can endure without daily contact. Divine love means daily contact in prayer. And, again, I'm not talking about some explosive earthquake-type of daily time with the Lord. I'm talking about simple, sincere, heartfelt prayer.

Did you ever hear the definition of prayer that comes to us from St. Teresa? She defined prayer as "nothing more than the friendly conversation in which the soul speaks heart-to-heart with the One we know loves us." You may recall the famous definition of prayer that Cardinal Newman gave us — *cor ad cor loquitor*, "heart speaking to heart."

I don't care what you call it. You can call it meditation; you can call it a quiet time with the Lord. And I don't care how you do it — Daily Mass, a Holy Hour, Rosary, reading the Gospels — but daily time with the Lord is essential if we're going to grow in our love of Jesus.

I remember how my mom and dad acted when I was growing up. They had such a loving relationship. My dad would get home from work around five each evening, dead tired. He would go and change, and then he would come into the kitchen, where Mom was putting the last-minute touches on the meal. For about an hour, Mom and Dad would just sit there, and we kids knew to leave them alone. That was their quality time together. Sometimes, they'd be in animated conversation. Sometimes, they wouldn't say anything. Dad might read the paper, and Mom might be peeling the potatoes. Sometimes, they might even be talking in a kind of heated way. There were a lot of different ways they'd spend that time, but they never missed that time together. And I'm convinced that's what increased the fervor of their love.

If we want to love Jesus, we want to spend time with Him every day in prayer. That's the first way.

Getting to Know the Lord

A second thing that will always enhance a relationship of love is getting to know the person better. I mentioned my brother Pat and Mary Theresa. Patrick was about thirty-five or thirty-six and wasn't married yet. Meanwhile, while I was in Rome, Mary Theresa Kelly called me. She was a girl from one of my former parishes who was then working as a radio announcer, and she wanted to find out how I was doing. We visited for a bit, and then she said, "Look, you've got to help me. The Pope is coming to St. Louis in January, and we want to start doing some stories, and I thought it would really be a coup if I could call a guy in Rome once a week and talk to him."

I replied, "Sure. I'll be happy to help, Mary Theresa. But how are you doing? How is your family? Are you married yet?"

She said, "No. I'm twenty-nine, and I've had some boyfriends, but my boyfriends drop me because they say all I want to do is go to Cardinal baseball games and drink beer!"

I laughed. "I've got a guy who would really like that. Could I have my brother call you?"

"Sure," she said.

Well, the rest is history. They're married now. They have two beautiful little girls — my nieces, Gracie and Kathleen — and my first nephew, Patrick.

But the point of this is, I knew their relationship was getting serious when Patrick began to ask me about her. He'd say, "Now, Tim, you know the family. What are they like? What was she like in high school? What are the mom and dad like? Where did she go to school?" He was so interested in her that he wanted to get to know more and more about her. We never lose that curiosity when we love somebody.

So, if we want to love Jesus more intensely, we have got to get to know Him better — and believe me, that's a lifelong task. The moment we think we know Him well, we're dead in the water. St. Paul tells us that His heart is of infinite riches and we can never, ever exhaust them.

Now, what does "getting to know Jesus better" mean? It means reading Scripture; it means reading the Catechism; it means spiritual reading. These are three tried-and-true ways that we get to know Jesus better: Scripture, theology, and spiritual reading.

I was talking to a priest recently about a book he was reading, and he said, "I always try to be reading something on the spiritual life, just to keep myself fresh." What a beautiful idea — that we never give up on reading, we never give up on Scripture, we never give up on theology. I tell this to the seminarians: "For you, theology is just not some dry science. For you, theology is an act of love and getting to know Jesus and His teaching better."

Pope John Paul II had a beautiful phrase — "theology on the knees" — meaning that he would very often study theology kneeling. It was a prayer for him. His theology then became spiritual reading.

One of the spiritual directors in a seminary where I was assigned used to call it "consecrated study." So that would be a way that we can spark our love for Jesus: Scripture, theology, and spiritual reading. We never give up on that. We keep it going our whole life.

SHARING A MEAL WITH OUR LORD

A third way we can grow in our relationship with Jesus is to sit at table with Him.

Often a couple starts moving toward "getting serious" when they go out for dinner. And you know that something *really* serious is going to happen if they go out for a really fancy, formal dinner! A meal is often an occasion for intensifying our love. This is also true for our love relationship with Our Lord.

The passage from the Gospel of John, at the beginning of this chapter, took place right after a meal. It's very interesting that almost all of Our Lord's post-Resurrection appearances take place in the context of a meal. In fact, my friends tease me that my favorite passage in all of Scripture, my favorite saying of Jesus, is when He appeared to His disciples after His Resurrection and said to them, "Does anybody have anything to eat?"

Our Lord loved a good meal. That was an occasion of friendship for Him. Obviously, then, for you and me, if we want to fortify our relationship of love with Jesus, that means we partake of the Eucharist. If we really want to fall in love with Our Lord or deepen our relationship with Him, we will have a meal with Him. And for us as Catholics, we have a sacred meal with Our Lord in the Holy Eucharist.

For us, the celebration of the Mass is the way Our Lord has chosen for us to sit down and share a meal with Him. To quote St. Pius X, "This side of Heaven, there's no more effective way of being in union with Jesus Christ than by reverently receiving Him in Holy Communion." Archbishop Sheen, when he was speaking to parish priests, would always say, "The barometer of the vitality of our spiritual life is how seriously we take our daily Mass." But this applies to all of us. Do we prepare for Mass? Do we participate with reverence and joy? Do we make a proper thanksgiving after it? Is it a source of nourishment for our souls? Is it the highlight of our day?

Just as a man and woman intensify their relationship by having a meal together, so do we grow in our love relationship with the Lord by sharing a meal with Him — the sacred banquet we call the Holy Sacrifice of the Mass.

Behold *Your* Mother

You know a man and a woman are getting serious about a relationship when they decide that it's time to meet each other's families, right? When he takes her to meet his parents, when she takes him to meet her parents and brothers and sisters? The same is true in our relationship of love with Our Lord. If we want to increase our love of Jesus, a good strategy on our part is to get to know His family. I am talking pre-eminently about His Mother.

A very effective and practical way to grow in our love for Jesus is to love His Mother. We have that great classical phrase in our Catholic spirituality, "To Jesus through Mary." Our Blessed Mother will always bring us closer to her divine Son.

There is a great passage from the masterpiece that Pope John Paul II wrote on his fiftieth anniversary, *A Priestly Ordination: Gift and Mystery*, in which he said that he came to a stage in his life as a seminarian when he realized that not only did Mary lead us to Jesus, but that Jesus also led us back to Mary. Our Lord knows that one of the tenderest, most effective ways that we can come to Him is through His own Blessed Mother.

Do you want to grow in your relationship with Our Lord? Do you want to be able to say with St. Peter, "Lord, You know everything. You know that I love You"? Then get to know His family. Get to know His Mother. Get to know the saints, who are members of the Communion of Saints, Our Lord's supernatural family.

I think of someone like St. Thérèse, the Little Flower of Jesus. When you read her works, you can't help but fall in love with Jesus! Getting to know her, a member of Our Lord's family, is a very effective way to grow in our love with Our Lord.

Apologizing to Our Lord

A fifth way that, with St. Peter, we can say, "Lord, You know everything; You know that I love You" is by learning to say "I am sorry." In my first parish assignment as a priest (I keep talking about that, it was such a happy experience being a parish priest), I was blessed with a great pastor, Msgr. Cornelius Flavan. Whenever Monsignor would have a wedding, he would look at the couple, beaming with excitement, and say, "Look, the six most important words you need for your marriage to work are these: 'I love you' are the first three, and the next three are 'I am sorry.'" He said, "If those two phrases, if those six words, characterize your conversation, your love will be strong and endure."

If we want to grow in our relationship with Our Lord, we will not only say to Him, "I love you"; we will also learn to say "I am sorry."

Do you know that some people think the reason Jesus asked Peter three times, "Do you love Me?" was to give him the chance to repent and to express contrition for the three times Peter had denied knowing Our Lord?

Remember, this episode comes to us after Our Lord's Resurrection. Our Lord wants to hear Peter say "I love you" because when we say "I love you," we have to say "I'm sorry." For us as Catholics, the way we tell Jesus we are sorry is through a good confession. I'd like to propose that you resolve to tell Our Lord "I love you" and "I'm sorry" frequently, in the sacrament of Penance.

I did a lot of work with priests and seminarians over the years I served as rector of North American College in Rome. During that time, I came to a conclusion. A real barometer of our love relationship with Our Lord is the frequency that we celebrate the sacrament of Penance.

Without fail, whenever a priest or a seminarian would say to me, "My life with Jesus is lackluster. Something is missing. I'm feeling lethargic and my spiritual life is drifting," almost unfailingly, the man had slipped away from the sacrament of Penance. Don't let that happen to you. Remember that for any relationship to flourish, "I love you" and "I am sorry" are necessary components, and we say both to Jesus through the sacrament of Penance.

It's a paradox in our Christian life that the more intensely we love Jesus, the more often we find ourselves saying, "I am sorry." Because we love Him so much, we are aware of the times we hurt Him. Mother Teresa used to go to Confession once a week. Pope John Paul II had a confessor that visited him every Friday. These were holy people! Some people might say, "The holier that we become, the more we're in love with Jesus, the less we need the sacrament of Penance." Are you kidding? The more we say "I love You, Lord," the more we feel the need to say "I am sorry."

Getting Rid of Whatever Hurts Him

Mary Theresa, from the beginning, hated a sweater that Patrick would wear. It began as a joke, and he would wear it just to get to her. But it got to the point where she said, "You know, Pat, I just hate that. Quit trying to get my Irish up. Get rid of it," and he did. He got rid of the sweater. He didn't want to damage his relationship with her; it wasn't worth it. Now, on the other hand, she drove him crazy with her shopping, because she wanted to shop all the time, and it hurt him that she wanted to shop all the time, and he let her know it. That, she didn't change.

But in general, if we know we're doing something or have some habit that we know hurts the other person — well, darn it, we get rid of it. Husbands and wives have to do this all the time to greater or lesser extents. This is what we mean by *metanoia*, what the Gospel translations often render as "repent." This is what we mean by conversion of heart. Jesus is constantly saying, "There are things in your life that have to go if you're going to be My disciple."

What is it? What is in my life that stands between me and Jesus? What is it in my life that hurts Him? What is it in my life that I need to purify so that I can love Him more? It might be a bad habit. It might be a vice, a sin, a relationship, a tendency, or a possession. There is something in my life that stands between Him and me. Just like Patrick wanted to get rid of that sweater because he knew it bothered Mary Theresa, we want to excise from our life anything that hurts the beloved. If we want to grow in our love of Jesus, we are to cleanse and purify anything in our life that hurts Him and blocks that love.

I love the encounter between Jesus and the rich young man. Remember? This guy was doing everything right. He comes up to Jesus and asks, "Master, what do I need to do?" He was asking a sincere question. "What do I need to do to gain eternal life?" And everything Jesus said he needed to do, the rich young man would say, "I'm doing it, I'm doing it, I'm doing it." Finally, Jesus looked hard at him and said, "Well, then go sell everything you have and give it to the poor and follow me," and the guy couldn't do it.

I remember one of the first retreats I ever went on as a seminarian. The retreat director used that passage and he asked each of us to meditate upon it, and I blew it off. I said, "Well, this certainly doesn't apply to me, because I don't have money. I don't have possessions. I don't have to meditate on this one." Most of the guys did the same thing, so it was a very pivotal moment when the retreat director said, "You missed the whole point. This isn't about the danger of riches. Jesus saw in his heart what was keeping that young man from totally following Him. In his case, it was riches. That might not be the case in your life, but you can bet your bottom dollar — if you had one — that there is something in your life Jesus will see when He looks at you that's got to go if you are to be His disciple."

The Christian life is always a turning toward something, meaning we're turning away from something else. It's a turning toward, and it's turning from. We usually don't have any problem turning toward Jesus, but we've got a big problem in leaving something behind. When people are falling out of love with Jesus, or when they admit that their love of Jesus is not as passionate as it should be, there is usually something in the soul that has got to go. That's a tough move, but we need to do it, because love is worth it.

SHARING INTERESTS WITH OUR LORD

Another way that we can intensify our love relationship with Our Lord is by sharing interests. We want to share interests with Jesus. What He cares about, we want to care about. A good sign with people falling in love is that they begin to share interests.

I knew things were getting serious between Pat and Mary Theresa when he went to a concert with her. I mean, my brother might go to a Garth Brooks concert, but he went to a real symphony, and I said, "Oh, this is serious, for my brother Pat to go to a symphony." And I knew, too, that things must be getting serious when she went bowling with him, because she didn't particularly care for bowling. But they loved each other enough that they knew they wanted to begin to share interests. That is very important in a relationship.

So it is with Our Lord.

If we want to grow in our love with Jesus, we want to share His interests. We want the things that are important to Him to be important in our life. And what are those? What were the things important to Our Lord? Who were the people He cared about and spent time with? You know the answer to that question — the poor, the sick, the suffering, the forgotten.

Jesus has a lot of interests, but there are two very special ones for us priests. First of all, the supreme interest of Jesus is in souls. Jesus loves souls. He wants to save every soul. So, for the priest, we would have the supreme interest in the soul. "Give me souls. Keep all the rest," as St. John Bosco said.

One day, a very beautiful woman came to see Fr. Solanus Casey. She was dressed rather immodestly, and her perfume filled the friary. All of the friars noticed her. She walked in, spoke to Fr. Solanus, and then left about an hour later. After she was gone, the other friars came up to Solanus and said, "Did you not see the way that lady was dressed? Did you not see the way that she looked?"

And what did Fr. Solanus say? He simply said, "All I saw was a soul."

His only concern was the soul. A good priest shares the concern of Our Lord for the souls of those to whom He entrusts us.

A second interest of Jesus that we would share is concern for people in need:

- the sick.
- the suffering.
- the sinner.
- the hungry.

- the prisoner.
- people in any need.
- the marginalized.

Have you ever noticed how Jesus was always aware of the people on the side of the road? When Jesus was walking the road, of course He's walking with friends, but His radar always goes up with those on the side of the road — whether it be Zacchaeus, or the woman hemorrhaging, or the blind man at the side of the road, whoever. He is always seeing those forgotten, left behind. That's an interest for Him, and it has to be an interest for us. Our antennae go up to people in need.

Those are two interests of Jesus that, if we make them our own, will deepend our love for Him.

If you want to grow in your love of Jesus, then you begin to spend time with the people He loves — the poor, the sick, the suffering, the forgotten. That's why an integral part of the spiritual life is the works of mercy and charity. Because if we're going to grow in our love with Our Lord, we're going to care about the people that He cares about.

A few years ago I was in Washington, DC, on January 22, for the annual Pro-life March. There, I met a young couple with two beautiful babies, who they told me were foster children. It turned out that this young couple is unable to have children of their own, but they're constantly taking in babies who have no place to go. They might be crack babies, abandoned babies, or sick babies, or babies who have a special need — and until those babies can be adopted, this young couple takes them in. Something tells me that this young couple loves Our Lord very much, because they're spending time with the people He loves.

Do you want to grow in your relationship with Our Lord? Share His interests. Spend time with the people He does — the poor, the sick, the lonely, the suffering.

Talk to Our Lord about the Future

We know that a man and a woman are getting serious when they start talking about sharing their future together — that's marriage — and sharing life together — that's bringing children into the world.

A very important quality in intensifying love is that people want to share life, and they want to share the future. This is what marriage is all about. When a relationship of love becomes marriage, that means a man and a woman want to literally share life and the future together. That's true for us priests as well. If our love for Jesus is going to be deep and fruitful, we will share life. For a married couple, that means children, doesn't it? For a priest, it means grace. We're just bursting to share it with others in Baptism, in the Anointing of the Sick, in the Eucharist, in preaching, in ministry to the poor, in the sacrament of Reconciliation.

We have the life of God in our soul, and we want to share it. We are bursting to share the life of Christ with others.

A married couple is always planning for the future — kids, house, savings, job, moving, always looking to the future. For all of us, when it comes to Our Lord, planning for the future means that we are planning on heaven. We should not be ashamed to say that we look forward to heaven. That's where our love for Jesus will be consummated. That's where it will be eternal. That's where it will be undistracted. We are not embarrassed to say we look forward to heaven. That's why, to use that beautiful phrase in aesthetical theology, you and I look at everything *sub specie eternitatis*, "in light of eternity." How is this going to help me get to heaven?

When he gives us his First Principle and Foundation in his *Spiritual Exercises*, St. Ignatius says that in every decision we have in life, there is only one question that we have to ask: "Is this going to help me save my soul, or is it going to distract me from saving my soul?" If it's going to help me get to heaven, I embrace it. If it's going to keep me from getting there, I throw it away, because everything is *sub specie eternitatis*, in light of eternity.

We want to be able to say with St. Peter, "Lord, You know everything; You know that I love You." We start thinking about spending eternity with the Lord. We're not afraid to speak of heaven! And we're not afraid to say, "Lord, I want to get to heaven and love You forever in eternity. And anything in this life that keeps me away from heaven, I don't want. And anything in this life that's going to help me reach heaven, bring it on, because I want it!"

It is just like those of you who are my age and older remember learning in the *Baltimore Catechism*: "Why did God make you? God made me to know Him, love Him and serve Him in this life, and to be happy with Him forever in the next." We want to spend forever with Jesus in heaven, so much do we love Him.

FAITHFUL TO THE END

The last characteristic would be exclusivity and fidelity. This doesn't apply to all of us in the natural plane. God willing, we're in love with a lot of people in very pure and chaste ways. We have wonderful friendships. But, of course, they never become exclusive for us. This is something that takes place only in marriage. In marriage, love between a husband and wife is faithful, fruitful, and forever; our relationship with Jesus has that quality. God is jealous of us. He wants us purely as His own.

He invites us to spend an unending future with Him. This is also true for those in sacred vows, in religious life, and for us priests.

I have a very good friend back home in St. Louis — she and I have been good friends for forty years — who is a woman religious and a remarkably good teacher. Sr. Rosario is the principal of a school now, but for the first twenty years that I knew her, she taught first grade. She was a dynamite first-grade teacher; she used to have special antennae for kids in trouble. She'd keep them after school to try to tutor them and show them some special love and care, especially if they came from broken families or violent homes.

One time, Sr. Rosario was spending some time with one little first-grade girl who she knew came from a terribly broken home, trying to help her learn to read better, when she noticed that the girl wasn't looking at the book. Instead, she was staring at Sr. Rosario. Finally, the little girl said, "Sister, are you married?"

Sr. Rosario replied, "No, honey, I'm not."

At that, the girl smiled and said, "Oh, good. That means you belong to all of us."

There is that definition of celibacy, or virginity, or chastity — that we belong exclusively to Jesus and His Church. He claims us totally as His own.

A priest to whom I was very close had a crisis in his life when he found himself falling in love with a woman, and he was very open and honest about it. I remember asking him, "Is it so severe that you're thinking of leaving the priesthood?"

And he said, "Tim, you know better than that. I am a priest from the top of my head to the tip of my toes. I could never be anything else."

He died not long ago, a very happy, faithful priest. That's what I mean by exclusively, totally, 100 percent belonging to Jesus and His Church.

Fr. Benedict Groeschel says it in his uniquely northern New Jersey way: "Celibacy means that we belong exclusively to the Lord, from our brain cells to our sperm cells." Everything belongs to God. We have given it all over to Jesus and His Church. That's the exclusivity and fidelity that Jesus expects from us. As Pope John Paul II used to say, "*Totus tuus* (We are all yours)." John Paul took that expression from the act of consecration of St. Louis de Montfort to the Blessed Mother.

SUMMARY

"Simon Peter, do you love Me?"

"Lord, You know everything; You know that I love You."

That's what we want to be able to say. "Lord, I love You so much. I want to love You even more, Lord! How can I love You more?"

I just gave you nine tips.

- We spend time with Him — that means prayer every day.
- We get to know Him better — that means learning more about Him through the Bible, the *Catechism*, and good spiritual reading.
- We take a meal with Him — that means the Eucharist, as often and as reverently as possible.
- We get to know His family, especially His Blessed Mother.
- We learn to say, "I am sorry" — especially in the sacrament of Penance.

- We clean from our life whatever hurts Him or whatever comes between Him and us — that's conversion of life; that's purity of heart.
- We share interests — that means we get to love the people He loves; namely, the poor, the suffering, the lonely, the forgotten.
- We begin to think about life together — that's grace. And forever together — that's heaven!
- We remain faithful to Him and His call in our life — we ultimately belong to Him alone.

7.

Duc in Altum —
"Put Out into the Deep"

And when Jesus had ceased speaking, he said to Simon, "Put out into the deep and let down your nets for a catch." And Simon answered, "Master, we toiled all night and took nothing! But at your word I will let down the nets." And when they had done this, they enclosed a great shoal of fish; and as their nets were breaking, they beckoned to their partners in the other boat to come and help them. And they came and filled both the boats, so that they began to sink. But when Simon Peter saw it, he fell down at Jesus' knees, saying," Depart from me, for I am a sinful man, O Lord." For he was astonished, and all that were with him, at the catch of fish which they had taken; and so also were James and John, sons of Zebedee, who were partners with Simon. And Jesus said to Simon, "Do not be afraid; henceforth you will be catching men." And when they had brought their boats to land, they left everything and followed him.

— Lk. 5:4-11

PUT OUT INTO THE DEEP
Have you ever heard the Latin phrase *duc in altum?* It means "put out into the deep," coming from the episode of St. Luke's Gospel quoted above. St. Peter received this order from the Master himself: *Duc in altum* — "Put out into the deep." I pro-

pose to you that Jesus is giving us the same exact imperative that He gave to St. Peter: *Duc in altum* — "Put out into the deep."

Jesus is not talking to us about fishing but about casting out into the depths of the spiritual life. Classically, this command has been interpreted as Our Lord's exhortation to perfection. All who wish to follow Him must be willing to "put out into the deep," to set aside human constraints and frustrations to pursue perfection.

Jesus is urging us to the depths of union with Him. He's urging us to be sanctified. He is calling us to heroic virtue! There can be nothing shallow, superficial, or halfway about our commitment to Him. It is deep, daring, and total. The summons to the deep, this call to perfection, is a constant theme in Our Lord's teaching.

Like our friend St. Peter, we might wish that Our Lord would leave well enough alone, but He won't. Every time in our spiritual lives — every time we seem to find a safe harbor where we might kind of just drift comfortably around for a while — He intrudes and tells us, "Put out into the deep — *Duc in altum.*"

Our Lord Expects More

Are you the oldest child in your family? I am, and I find myself a little bit more sympathetic, or at least understanding, of this imperative of Our Lord. We older children are more used to this prodding of Jesus toward perfection. When I was growing up, I heard this so many times! I'd be in the same room with my brothers, Bob and Patrick, and the room would be messy. Bob and Pat might be let off the hook, but not me. "You are the oldest," mom and dad would say to me. "We expect more out of you."

In a way, that's what Our Lord is saying to St. Peter, and that's what He's saying to us. "Put out into the deep. Nothing shallow. Nothing halfway. I expect more out of you."

Do you remember the Sermon on the Mount? Recall when Our Lord keeps saying over and over again, "But I say unto you..." He keeps repeating that. He says, "Compromise, accommodation, wavering, getting by with the least demanding, and obedience to the letter rather than the spirit of the law — that might have characterized all of you up until now, but I say unto you, if you are going to be My disciple, I expect perfection. I expect sanctity. I expect heroic virtue. Be perfect, as your heavenly Father is perfect."

How much more blunt can you get than that? And He doesn't want any whimpering, like we find from our friend St. Peter in this Gospel passage. We don't want any wavering. We don't want excuses. We don't want to be like St. Peter, saying, "Oh, Lord, I've done enough. Can't we just give it a rest?"

"No," Our Lord says. "*Duc in altum* — put out into the deep."

Like Peter, let's be honest, we sometimes get a little exhausted, frustrated, and discouraged. At times, we prefer the shallow water, where it's safer, easier, and closer to the shore. But the orders keep coming. "I say unto you, 'Put out into the deep. *Duc in altum.*' Be perfect, as my heavenly Father is perfect. I call you to perfection, to sanctity, to heroic virtue."

BE GOOD; I KNOW YOU CAN BE

I remember once seeing the late Cardinal John O'Connor surrounded by reporters on TV, being hammered with questions about his opposition to a plan for the widespread distribution of condoms in public schools to curb AIDS and teenage pregnancy. One of the reporters stuck a microphone in Cardinal

O'Connor's face and said, "Cardinal, you're expecting an awful lot from people, especially our young people, in thinking they can control themselves. That's an awfully high standard. Isn't it just better to admit that people can't live up to this so they have to take precautions?"

Do you know what the Cardinal replied? "Oh, no," he said to the reporter. "The whole world is saying to our young people, 'Be good, but — wink, wink — we know you can't, so at least be careful.' Somebody has got to say, 'Be good; I know you can be,' and that has to be the Church."

Duc in altum: "Put out into the deep."

OUR LORD LIFTS US UP

In his magnificent *Life of Christ,* the great Archbishop Sheen reflects on one of Our Lord's promises: "When I am lifted up . . ." [Jesus meant when He was lifted up on the cross], ". . . I will draw all men to myself." Archbishop Sheen points out that that idea happens to violate laws of nature — the law of gravity, to be precise — because in nature, all falls down. Everything is forced down to the earth by gravity.

Yet here, Jesus is saying, "No! I will draw all things up to myself." To be drawn up to Jesus through sanctity, through the pursuit of perfection and heroic virtue, goes against all the heavy forces of nature that are there to drag us down. While Jesus is calling us upward, while Jesus is calling us to the deep, the world drags us downward and says, "Stay in the shallow."

ARE YOU A BOBO?

Have you ever heard of the book by David Brooks with the catchy title *Bobos in Paradise*? I finished it awhile back, and it's worth the read. Brooks argues that today's ruling elite (he's talking about the dot-com millionaires, the airbrush politicians, the celebrity pundits, the media empire builders, along with millions of educated beneficiaries of our booming information economy) "constitute a new social class" that he calls *bourgeois bohemians*, or Bobos.

What Brooks argues is that in their manners and belief, these folks combine the 1960s' bohemian values of self-expression, pleasure-seeking, and a general distrust of authority, with the 1980s' bourgeois values of selfish consumerism. According to the author, Bobos aren't looking to be called to any higher moral ground. They don't expect an America that's a shining city on the hill. All they want is a comfortable, cozy, convenient, tolerant complacency.

The Bobo doesn't ask, "What does the Lord expect of me?" Rather, he is more likely to ask "What will the Lord do for me? How will the Lord meet my needs?"

As Brooks sums it up, "They just aim at being decent, not being saints. They prefer a moral style that doesn't shake things up."

Well, sorry, Bobos, but we happen to have a Lord who enjoys shaking things up, who loathes the shallow water, who nudges us, actually *nags* us, to put out into the deep. And perhaps in a more pointed way, Jesus and His Church, and even the world, expect from us a depth, a sanctity, a heroic virtue, a pursuit of perfection. They expect us to put out into the deep.

WAYS TO GO DEEPER — PRAYER

What are some ways that we can join St. Peter in putting out into the deep?

The first is, guess what? Prayer. The Fathers of the Church, the great thinkers of the first four or five centuries of the Church, often interpreted Our Lord's injunction to St. Peter,

Duc in altum, as a summons to foster the depths of the interior life, by plumbing the depths and the richness of Christ himself.

This is a call to sanctity. It's an invitation to know and love Jesus at the very depth of our being. It is the task of developing a durable, sustaining, interior life, a rich, personal relationship with Our Lord that can only come from a daily conversation with Him in prayer — that's a primary duty of anyone interested in real, genuine discipleship.

Remember what St. Bernard said? "If you were wise you would first be reservoirs, and then channels."

Do you see what St. Bernard means? We are often channels — we are doing this, we' re doing that, we're giving this, we're giving that, we're going here and we're going there. Channels! Certainly, all good stuff. But St. Bernard says, "First, you'd better have the reservoir." You had better take care of the reservoir deep down in your soul and make sure that it is filled up with the life-giving waters that only Jesus Christ can give us, or else the reservoir is going to be empty and the channels are going to be dry.

The life insurance policy of making sure that the reservoir never goes empty is prayer. Keep in mind what happens in the Gospel. It was only after St. Peter put out his nets into the deep waters that he caught the miraculous draft of fish. So, too, it's only after we tend to the depths of our soul — our interior life — by plumbing the depths of the Heart of Christ that we can be zealous, committed, faithful disciples of Our Lord and Savior Jesus Christ. The way that this can be done is through daily, disciplined prayer.

WAYS TO GO DEEPER — "NEVER TIRE OF DOING GOOD"
A second area where we can put out into the deep — and let me borrow a phrase here from St. Peter's fellow apostle, St.

Paul — is "Never tire of doing good." St. Paul tells us this in two places, once in Romans and the other time in Galatians: "Never tire of doing good."

Let's admit it, for you and for me as disciples of Christ, every once in a while we get tired, discouraged, a little down. We get fatigued with doing good works. We feel like saying to Our Lord, "Can't we stop? Can't this service, can't this love, can't this pursuit of perfection, can't this constantly doing good and trying to lead virtuous, upright, saintly lives — can't we take a little break? Can't we just tread water for while? Can't we just stay here in the shallow water and take a nap?"

Of course, Our Lord says, "No! Put out into the deep. *Duc in altum.* Never tire of doing good."

One of the most touching descriptions we have of Jesus in the pages of the Gospel is when the evangelist tells us that He "went about doing good." Isn't that a simple description of the life and ministry of Jesus? He went about doing good. You and I are supposed to imitate Him. That means you and I are supposed to go about doing good. But periodically we want to lock the door and turn off the phone; we don't want to go to the committee meeting, help the poor, do our service project — we're tired of being kind and compassionate and smiling. Every once in a while, we want to say, "Enough!" But, as Blessed Columba Marmion says, "'Enough' is not a word found in the Christian vocabulary, because we never tire of doing good in our casting out into the deep."

Ways to Go Deeper — Fostering a Horror of Sin

A third practical way that we can strive for this perfection that Jesus encourages St. Peter (and us) toward: developing a horror of sin. All sin — obviously, mortal sin, deadly sin, but I'm also talking about venial sin. In our life of perfection, in our pursuit of sanctity and heroic virtue, we dread sin, all sin!

To this day I remember the story I heard for the first time in second grade, about St. Dominic Savio. Do you remember the little fourteen-year-old saint? Do you remember the motto that guided his life, "Death rather than sin"? That's how much he dreaded sin, this young boy on the road to perfection.

The one who takes seriously Our Lord's call to the deep, daily strives to fight sin. He or she is always at work on a particular one, and he or she frequently examines his or her conscience to let the light of God's grace show the "streaks." We are constantly on the fight against sin.

I remember being in Rome right before the canonization of Philadelphian St. Katharine Drexel, the great apostle to the African-Americans and Native Americans, when a reporter called me from United States and interviewed me. He said, "Monsignor, all these beatifications and canonizations that the Pope is doing — isn't all this goodness and holiness and virtue unrealistic and impossible today?"

I replied, "Listen. The pope's point is just the opposite! The pope's point is that such goodness, holiness, and virtue are possible — and not only possible, but expected, in those who claim to follow Christ."

The horror of sin never discourages us, but it inspires us to more sanctity. We never give in, we never give up in our fight against sin. And it's never going to end until we're six feet under.

"Let them know no limit to spiritual progress nor to likeness to God," suggests St. Gregory Nazianzen in his exegesis on this passage, *Duc in altum*. Jesus expects us to be on the road to sanctity, in pursuit of perfection, heroic in our virtue.

A Few Warnings

First of all, in our pursuit of perfection, we must never, ever get arrogant. Never does our putting out into the deep waters turn us into self-righteous, pious frauds, comfortable in our presumed identity as "holier than thou."

Msgr. Martin Helreigel, a legendary priest from the Archdiocese of St. Louis, remarked, "We are to have our head in the clouds, yes; but we are to have our feet firmly planted on the earth; and we are to have our heart on the Cross." So, we are never arrogant, never "holier than thou."

A second thing we've got to be careful about is discouragement. I'm giving you quite a plateful in this chapter. Simply put, I'm challenging you to be a saint, to be perfect, to be intimate with God. Now my friends, that's a lifelong task, and we can't do it unless we have humility and perseverance.

Mother Teresa said, "God doesn't ask us to be successful. He asks us to be faithful." The Lord wants us to keep trying, to persevere, to be humble, to be faithful, and to never give up.

A third area that we've got to be careful about is to never forget that it is the Lord, not the hard work of the fishermen, accomplishing the great task. It's only when St. Peter said to Jesus, "Lord, this is useless! We've been at it all night. We can't do anything else; but if You say so, I'll put out into the deep." It's only then that the miracle occurred, okay?

Holiness, sanctity, the pursuit of perfection — it's all God's doing, it's the Lord's doing, not ours. We can't win it, achieve it, or earn it. He does it through us, in us, and often, in spite of us.

Mary as Our Model

Our Blessed Mother Mary powerfully mirrors that perfection, that sanctity, and that virtue to which her Son summons us. In her Immaculate Conception, the Creator reminds us that sin-*lessness*, not sin-*fulness*, was His original blueprint for humanity. In her Annunciation, the tragedy of the Garden of Eden is rewound, as the New Eve obeys and cancels the disobedience of the first. Through her Assumption, the Lord recalls that life, not death, was His intention for us from the beginning.

The world will tell you that sanctity, the pursuit of perfection, and heroic virtue are frustrating, silly, and impossible! But I say to you, the world is wrong!

Our Lord expects more out of us. But from the beginning, this was not so. Because we are created in the image and likeness of God, we are redeemed by the precious Blood of His only-begotten Son, we are baptized into His life, we are fed with His very Body and Blood, we are destined for eternal union with Him. So, we don't stay onshore. We don't stay in shallow waters. With St. Peter, we put out into the deep.

8.

ASKING OUR LORD FOR
FORGIVENESS

And as Peter was below in the courtyard, one of the maids of the high priest came; and seeing Peter warming himself, she looked at him, and said, "You also were with the Nazarene, Jesus." But he denied it, saying, "I neither know nor understand what you mean." And he went out into the gateway. And the maid saw him, and began again to say to the bystanders, "This man is one of them." But again he denied it. And after a little while again the bystanders said to Peter, "Certainly you are one of them; for you are a Galilean." But he began to invoke a curse on himself and to swear, "I do not know this man of whom you speak." And immediately the cock crowed a second time. And Peter remembered how Jesus had said to him, "Before the cock crows twice, you will deny me three times." And he broke down and wept.

— Mk. 14:66-72

PETER'S DENIAL

This story of St. Peter's denial of Our Divine Lord can teach us something very important about the beauty and the power of the sacrament of Penance. I want you to think seriously about the sacrament of Penance. Let's put it into context, shall we? Imagine for a moment the horror of Peter's sin. Just on the face of it — to think that he would deny even knowing the

121

Savior of the World — that's a hideous sin for any believer. But how the ugliness of Peter's sin is even more intense! Think about it.

For one, it's not as if St. Peter broke down under some severe torture, or even before the threat of punishment. The one who asks him if he knows the man from Nazareth is not some brute soldier or menacing thug; she's not a torturer turning the rack or a judge ready to sentence, but a harmless cleaning woman.

Then the circumstances — Peter denies Jesus at the time Our Lord is most alone, most in trouble, most in need of a friend, at the time of His sacred Passion. Peter denies Him and fails to show his loyalty at this most critical time.

A third circumstance added to the gravity of Peter's sin: Peter had sworn up and down that he would never abandon Jesus. Recall his bold, daring words, "Lord, we will go to Jerusalem with You to suffer." Remember at the Last Supper, when Peter said, "Lord, just tell me who it is who will betray You; I'll take care of him." Instead, strong, courageous Peter was reduced to quivering jello in front of some teenage maid, when you think he would have been prepared.

Jesus had actually told Peter — had warned him — that he would betray Him! So one would think that Peter would have been ready to resist such a temptation as denying Our Lord.

Of all people, maybe someone who had barely known Jesus could be excused for denying Christ — but Peter? The one who had heard His teaching, beheld His miracles, witnessed His divinity, grown to know and love His Master . . . and who had been prepared for the horror of the Passion of Christ by witnessing the glory of His Transfiguration? And finally, to stumble impetuously and deny Our Lord one time — maybe, maybe we could excuse that. But again and again? Breaking finally into curses and swearing that he never even heard of this Man, Jesus?

Imagine the horror of Peter's sin. Imagine the depth of Peter's self-loathing when he heard that cock crow and realized that Jesus had actually foretold his denial. Think of how everything must have come crashing in on him. In the utterly simple words of the Gospel, "Peter went out and wept bitterly."

THE SCARS OF SIN

While I was in Rome as Rector of the North American College, I learned to appreciate the work of the great Italian artist, Michelangelo Merisi, better known as Caravaggio, who often portrayed St. Peter in his famous paintings. There is one of the Crucifixion of St. Peter on which, if you look closely at the face of Peter, you see that it is etched with deep furrows. The story goes that someone asked Caravaggio, "Why did you paint St. Peter with these deep furrows in his face?"

Caravaggio responded, "Because he wept so intensely after he denied Jesus three times that those tears permanently scarred his face."

Of course, that's the point. Here we have a drama of grievous, hideous sin, followed by acknowledgment, sorrow, and renewal. Because the point is not the horror of the sin, as bad as it was; the point is the recovery of the sinner. I'm speaking to you of resilient repentance.

I like that phrase, "resilient repentance." I propose to you that Peter can teach us resilient repentance.

You bet Peter sinned viciously — but then, he admitted his sin. He repented through powerful tears. He recovered. Peter knew his Lord so well that he realized mercy was his for the asking. Peter knew his Lord so well that he recognized that the Man he had just denied even knowing was suffering and dying precisely to forgive that hideous sin that he just committed.

St. Peter and Judas Iscariot

How different Peter's reaction to his sin was than that of another apostle — namely, Judas Iscariot.

Think about it: both men sinned grievously. Peter denied Jesus three times; Judas sold Him for thirty pieces of silver. Both men were warned about their sin by Jesus himself before they committed it. Both Peter and Judas had all the advantages of knowing Our Lord intimately through years of faithful discipleship. Their sin was similar, but their reactions were so different.

Judas dwelt on guilt, Peter on mercy. Judas thought he could never be forgiven; Peter knew better. Judas felt he could never go on; Peter realized he had to. Judas believed his sin stronger than the forgiveness of God; Peter knew nothing was stronger than the mercy of God. Judas turned inward on himself; Peter turned outward to Jesus. Judas took a rope and hanged himself; Peter was the first at the empty tomb that Easter morning, first of the apostles to preach on Pentecost, the one to lead the infant Church. Peter knew his Lord so well that he recognized that no sin, even one as hideous as his own, was outside the realm of Divine Mercy.

I'm talking about the resilient repentance of Peter verses the ruinous remorse of Judas Iscariot.

Peter's Testimony

It's moving to realize that the poignant story of Peter's triple denial of Our Lord could have been told by only one person. Think about it. How have we come to know the story of

Peter's denial of Our Lord? There is only one person who could have told us, and that is St. Peter himself.

I find it very moving to picture St. Peter, in that first generation of the Church, sharing with his brothers and sisters the story of his own sin and the story of his resilient repentance — what the mercy of God can do!

This admission, mercy, and renewal take place for us specifically, powerfully, and dramatically in the sacrament of Penance. For us, as for St. Peter, the forgiveness of Christ is not some vague, impersonal theory. It's a precise, one-on-one, down-to-earth sacramental moment. It takes place in Confession. There, like St. Peter, we acknowledge our sin. There, like the fisherman, we believe in the overwhelming power of God's mercy. There, like Simon Peter, we are renewed and we get on with our life.

I've been a priest now for a lot of years, and I've learned that if we admit that we're in a period of spiritual lassitude or a time of lethargy in our life of faith — if we admit that our relationship with Jesus Christ is not what it should be — odds are we have drifted away from the sacrament of Penance. The sacrament of Penance is a magnificently effective and powerful way to rekindle our devotion to Our Lord.

AVOIDING THE EXTREMES

This sacrament of Penance is a very practical way to keep us in the "healthy middle" with St. Peter. What do I mean by the "healthy middle"?

In our moral life, our life of responding to the moral demands of Our Lord, there are two extremes that we have to avoid.

On the one hand is the extreme of the Pharisees, who felt they were sinless, and therefore needed no forgiveness. I'm afraid the stance of the Pharisees is the posture of many people today, even some of our faithful Catholic people. "Oh, I don't have any sin. Everything is okay with me. Sin is really just some outdated notion. I'm okay, you're okay. I have no sin. Thus, I really need no forgiveness from the Lord. So why go to the sacrament of Penance?"

This is the extreme of the Pharisees. It is a presumption that God's mercy is there and we can take it for granted or ignore it, because we don't need it. However, it's hard to fall into that extreme if we're faithful to the sacrament of Reconciliation.

The other extreme is that of Judas, who felt his sin was so severe that he could never be forgiven. That is despair. This is the opposite of the person who presumes on God's mercy.

Despair will never be ours if we believe in the power of the sacrament of Penance and tap into it very often. This sacrament helps us avoid both extremes — the presumption of the Pharisees and the despair of Judas — and it keeps us, with St. Peter, in a healthy center. Contrite? Yes, but confident in the Lord's mercy. Aware of the sin? You bet, but equally aware of Christ's desire to forgive. Repentant? You bet, but renewed as well. And for us, this moment of honesty and healing takes place, concretely and personally, in the sacrament of Penance.

I want to be blunt. I am a meat-and-potato guy; there's nothing real complicated, nothing really exotic, about any of this stuff that I've been telling you. One of the best ways we can insure that we are walking with Our Lord is through a very sincere, honest, humble celebration of the sacrament of Penance.

I know a lot of you have been away from this sacrament for a long time. The sad statistics tell us that. So what better gift can we give to the Lord than to join St. Peter in that resilient repentance and tell Our Lord that His Passion and Death were worthwhile, that we need to be bathed in His Precious Blood, that we need the mercy and forgiveness that He won for us that Good Friday on the Cross? What better gift can we give Him than to make that repentance personal, sacramental, one-on-one, and down-to-earth in the faithful celebration of the sacrament of Penance?

THE REVITALIZATION OF THE SACRAMENT OF PENANCE

I've mentioned to you that I had the blessing of spending seven years in Rome as Rector of the Pontifical North American College. I had the added blessing of being there for the great Jubilee Year, the year 2000. A lot of people say to me, "Bishop Dolan, what do you most remember of the Jubilee Year? What sticks in your mind? What seemed to be the most dramatic event?"

No doubt about it, I can answer that readily and sincerely. It wasn't one event; it was something I witnessed for the entirety of the Jubilee Year, and that was the tremendous return to the sacrament of Penance.

Before the Jubilee, the priests and the seminarians that lived in Rome would often go down to St. Peter's Basilica for the sacrament of Penance and usually, there might be two or three people in line in front of you. You could go down to St. Peter's, spend some moments in preparation, make your good Confession and a prayer of thanksgiving, and be back up to the College in forty or forty-five minutes.

But not during the Jubilee Year! We used to tease one another and say, "Boy, we will be glad when this year is over, because you can't get to Confession anymore." You saw hundreds and hundreds of people going to Confession. You'd go into St. Peter's, into John Lateran, into Mary Major, into St.

Paul Outside the Walls, or one of the other great temples in the Eternal City, and there you would see lines of people in the sacrament of Penance, all accepting the Holy Father's challenge to use this great Jubilee Year as a time of interior renewal, conversion of heart, and return to the Lord's mercy through the sacrament of Reconciliation.

I remember during the great World Youth Day in Rome, you couldn't walk down Via della Conciliazione without young people stopping you to say, "Father, do you speak English? Would you hear my Confession?" I sat for nine hours at Circus Maximus, where they had confessionals set up for the hundreds of thousands of young people from every language who had come from throughout the world.

I remember going into St. Peter's Basilica, having people stop me, and just walking with them over to the pillars because they wanted to return to the sacrament of Penance.

I recall on the Thursday after Ash Wednesday of the Jubilee Year, walking into St. Peter's Basilica myself to go to Confession. I found it jammed with thousands of priests, priests of the Diocese of Rome, who had come on this Thursday after Ash Wednesday to be with their bishop — who happens to be our Holy Father, the Pope, the bishop of Rome — for a morning of recollection. Priests were going to Confession, one to another. Every corner you looked at in the Basilica, there were priests.

And I thought, "What a moment of triumph! What a moment of grace for the Church! The devil is on the run! Sin is being defeated! The Passion, death, and Resurrection of Jesus Christ are being applied during this great Jubilee Year."

Without a doubt, to see that return and that renewal in the sacrament of Penance during that great Jubilee Year was, for me, the high point of the year.

THE GREATEST SUFFERING OF BLESSED DAMIEN OF MOLOKAI

It makes me think of the story of Blessed Damien the Leper. Perhaps you have heard this story. Blessed Damien the Leper served the lepers on the Hawaiian Island of Molokai and eventually contracted leprosy himself. But it might surprise you to know what the greatest suffering that Blessed Damien experienced was.

Was it being away from family and friends for decades?

Was it the slander and the lack of charity that he had to face when people accused him of sexual immorality — because at that time, they thought that was the only way you could contract leprosy? Was it having to bear those malicious rumors?

Was it the physical suffering of being a leper himself? Remember the story of Blessed Damien's housekeeper bringing in the steaming pot of tea and tripping and spilling it on Damien's feet? She gasps and starts to apologize, then realizes that Damien didn't even feel it because of his leprosy. His feet and his legs were dead. Was it that physical suffering that was most difficult for Damien to bear?

No, it wasn't any of these that was his worst suffering. Blessed Damien the Leper tells us that his heaviest cross was the inability to approach the sacrament of Penance frequently.

No priest would come to Molokai, so when Blessed Damien would hear that ships were coming in, he would go down to the docks to meet them. Other people were going down for tobacco, letters, medicine, and tea. But none of these was his interest; he would stand on the dock and ask, "Is there a priest on board?" And every once in awhile, a priest would come out, as far as to the plank, but wouldn't leave the ship for fear of contagion. So Damien would make his Confession right there. He would shout up from the dock in Latin or in Flemish, so the other people couldn't understand him, and make his Confession.

His greatest suffering was the inability to frequently approach the sacrament of Penance.

Make Use of the Sacrament

We don't have Blessed Damien's problem — we've got the sacrament of Penance at our doorstep. There is not a parish in the United States that doesn't offer the sacrament of Penance on a regular basis. Let's take Our Lord at His word, join St. Peter in that resilient repentance, and let Our Lord wash our feet in this powerful sacrament.

Remember the words of Archbishop Sheen: "To be a sinner is our greatest curse; to admit it is our greatest blessing." And that takes place in the sacrament of Penance.

9.

TO WHOM SHALL WE GO?

"It is the spirit that gives life, the flesh is of no avail; the words that I have spoken to you are spirit and life. But there are some of you that do not believe." For Jesus knew from the first who those were that did not believe, and who it was that would betray him. And he said, "This is why I told you that no one can come to me unless it is granted him by the Father." After this many of his disciples drew back and no longer went about with him. Jesus said to the twelve, "Do you also wish to go away?" Simon Peter answered him, "Lord, to whom shall we go? You have the words of eternal life; and we have believed, and have come to know, that you are the Holy One of God." Jesus answered them, "Did I not choose you, the twelve, and one of you is a devil?" He spoke of Judas the son of Simon Iscariot, for he, one of the twelve, was to betray him.

— Jn. 6:63-71

AD QUEM IBIMUS — TO WHOM SHALL WE GO?
This has to be one of St. Peter's finer moments. We can't take that away from him. Just think of the power, the tenderness, the love, the utter honesty of that heartfelt, moving prayer. "Lord, to whom shall we go? You have the words of everlasting life."

I don't know if I'm reading anything into this or not, but it's almost as if I detect a note of exasperation in Peter's voice. Picture the context of this prayer of St. Peter. It comes at the end of that poetic sixth chapter of St. John's gospel, the famous Eucharistic discourse, that uplifting but tough teaching on the Eucharist and on eternal life. Until then, many people had been sympathetic to the message of Jesus. But after hearing this, they departed from Him because, to use the words of St. John, they found this language intolerable. And it's at that moment when you can't help but feel sorry for Jesus: He's watching people walk away from Him after He has just given them that magnificent promise of the Eucharist and of life eternal. So He turns to His apostles and says, "Do you also wish to go away?"

This pitiable plea from the heart of Jesus prompts that magnificent reply of Peter: "Lord, to whom shall we go? You have the words of everlasting life." But I wonder if Peter's actually almost pleading, "You know, Lord . . .

"Most of the time, we don't understand what You're teaching, either.

"Most of the time, it goes over our heads.

"Most of the time, we can't make much sense out of it.

"Most of the time, we find Your teachings difficult and demanding.

"Yes, there have been times that we've been tempted to walk away because You just don't seem to make any sense.

"But Lord, we don't care. You're all we've got. We have come to love You, believe in You, hope in You; and we have come to know that even though we don't always understand You, and even though You at times confuse, frustrate, and exasperate us, we know that You have the words of everlasting life. There is nowhere else to go. We are in it for the long haul."

I don't know if I'm reading too much into it. All I know is that exasperation in the voice of Peter makes a lot of sense to me because I've been there before, and I think you have, too.

This verse from St. John's Gospel happens to be my Episcopal motto: "To whom shall we go (*Ad quem ibimus*)?" I don't mind telling you how I got that. In September of the year 2000, my little nine-year-old niece, Shannon, was diagnosed with terribly aggressive cancer. It was a very difficult time, exacerbated because I was away from home, and you know how you exaggerate things when you're far away. I kept thinking *they're not telling me the whole thing*. And to some degree, that was probably true — although they did speak to me openly about how crushing the chemotherapy was on her, how she was in danger of losing her leg or even her life, and how the surgery was very delicate. When I talked to her on the phone, even though she was nauseated and in pain, she never complained, which made it almost tougher on us because our hearts just went out to her.

Not knowing what else to do, I would just pray hard. I would go down to the little chapel at the North American College, the Blessed Sacrament Chapel, and say, "Lord, it doesn't make much sense." I'd plead: "Do it to me, but why are you doing it to Shannon? She's barely nine years old. She's got her whole life ahead of her. She's such an innocent, beautiful little girl. I don't understand it at all, Lord." I'd pray like that. I'd just talk turkey to the Lord. I'd seek consolation. And I don't mind telling you, not much came.

It didn't help that right next door to the college — literally a nine-iron shot away — is Bambino Gesu Hospital, the children's hospital in Rome. So as I would be sitting there praying for Shannon, with the windows open, guess what I would be hearing? Babies crying. Or worse, mothers and fathers crying. Sometimes when I'd get up to close the window, because I couldn't take that crying anymore, I would look outside. One time when I was doing this, I saw a father carrying a little casket out of the hospital. So that didn't help. Here I'm seeking consolation, and *this* is what I get.

In the midst of that exasperation, I can remember settling upon this magnificent, gripping prayer of St. Peter. I found myself whispering, "Lord, this doesn't seem to be the way to run a railroad. I don't know where justice, compassion, and Your promised healing is in all this, but Lord, You are all I've got. To whom else shall I go? You and You alone have the words of everlasting life, and I'm in it for the long haul. I believe that You're in charge here and that You are Lord. And while it doesn't make much sense with You, it would make absolutely no sense at all without You. So, Lord, to whom else shall I go?" *Ad quem ibimus.*

So that summer, when I was told I was to be auxiliary bishop of St. Louis and advised to pick an Episcopal motto, no more than three words of some Scripture, I had absolutely no problem. *Ad quem ibimus.* "To whom shall we go?"

Christ and His Church

Thatis why that prayer makes so much sense to me. Let me take it one step further. I've already asked you to bear with me as I interpret this Scripture passage to express a hint of exasperation from Peter. I want to stretch it a bit further because for you and me, as believers, as Catholics, Jesus is alive, present, and active in His Church. The Church is His mystical body. It is a package deal for you and for me. There is no separating Christ from His Church. So when we say with Peter, "Lord, to whom shall we go?" we also add "You and Your

Church." "You and Your Church" have the words of everlasting life. I ask you to think long and hard about it, because you talk about a tough teaching? That's a very unpopular one today.

You may be familiar with Fr. Ron Rolheiser, the columnist. I admire him immensely. He claims it used to be said — what, thirty or thirty-five years ago? — that we lived in a post-Christian era. Remember? Now he says, "Forget it." We don't live in a post-Christian era now. Jesus is popular. Everybody loves Jesus. Today, we live in a post-Church era; now, we have believers but not "belongers." We have people who want a king without a kingdom. People want Jesus Christ, but not His Church. But for us Catholics, that cleavage is impossible, because Christ and His Church are one.

We place great stock in the words of Jesus to Saul on the Road to Damascus. "Saul, Saul, why are you persecuting Me?" He didn't say, "Why are you persecuting My people? Why are you persecuting My Church?" Jesus thundered, "Why are you persecuting Me?" He and His Church are synonymous. If we're trying to ask ourselves "What is the Church?" we're asking the wrong question. We should be asking, "Who?" Who is the Church? Christ is the Church.

Msgr. Flavin, to whom I have referred often in this book, was a great convert maker. He always began his instructions by saying, "A theist is somebody who believes in God; a Christian is a theist who believes that Jesus is the Son of God; and a Catholic is a Christian who believes that Jesus is alive in His Church."

Just as Peter found it somewhat exasperating to love Christ, so do we find it — let's be honest — so do we find it exasperating, at times, to love the Church.

Flannery O'Connor, the great southern Catholic novelist, wrote, "It's not suffering for the Church that bothers me; it's suffering from her." Or as Mary Settle, another renowned southern Catholic literary critic, wrote to Walker Percy, the physician-turned-novelist who converted to Catholicism: "Congratulations, but get ready. It's a rather untidy outfit you're joining up with." She was right. The Church, in her human side, is indeed imperfect, messy, corrupt, unjust, sinful, and untidy.

Dorothy Day, the founder of the Catholic Worker movement — herself a convert to Catholicism — said, "The Church is at times a spotless bride of Christ and at other times she is the whore of Babylon, but we love her to death because she is Christ and she has the words of everlasting life." Fr. Rolheiser says, "The Church is always God hung between two thieves."

THE CHURCH: THE SAME YESTERDAY AND TODAY

When I was a seminarian I was away in Rome for four years, but we came home our second summer to do some intensive pastoral work back in our home dioceses. I was assigned to my home parish, at the pastor's request, and it was a wonderful summer. I was close to my family and I loved my pastor, and he put me to work. One of my tasks was to bring Holy Communion to the sick. Among those I visited in the parish were Bill and Lena.

Bill and Lena were dynamic, nice-looking, and had a wonderful family. But, although they were only in their mid-thirties, Lena developed rheumatoid arthritis and became literally crippled. She was still beautiful, but she was curled up in a kind of a fetal position, and in constant pain.

I would bring her Holy Communion on Fridays, and I always admired how Bill tended to her. In the morning, he would get her out of bed, bathe her, dress her, and feed her. He'd return home in the afternoon to visit with her and feed her lunch. In the evening he would comb her hair, chat with her, and feed her again. They were very much in love, and I admired that so much. He was a big, strapping, handsome guy. She was no longer sexually fulfilling to him. She couldn't be. There is no way they could experience that aspect of marriage, but their love was so evident. I remember once saying to Bill as I left, "Bill, I just want you to know how much I admire your love for her." And he said to me, "Tim, she is more beautiful to me today than she was on the day I married her."

I thought, *My Lord, what love can do.* And, of course, that's the way we are with the Church. Sometimes she is a sparkling, radiant bride, walking down the aisle, and other times she's curled up in bed, helpless, painful, of no satisfaction to us, but we love her all the more. When the Church is crippled and bedridden, when she is weak and helpless, that's when she needs us most and when our love is most pure. And I guess it's true that at times the man we love so much, Jesus, can seem distant, confusing, and frustrating; at times, His Bride and ours, the Church, can also seem corrupt, weak, mistaken, scandalous, out of it. Well, that's when we love Him and her all the more. That's when love proves itself.

Not too long ago, a struggling priest said to me, "You know, Archbishop, I'm having big trouble because the Church that I was ordained for is no longer the Church I see today." I replied, "You're wrong. It's the same Church. Many men who have been married thirty, thirty-five, forty years can say, 'You know, she's not the same woman I married.' So what's he going to say? 'I'm leaving her'? No. [He says] 'I love her all the same. In substance she's the same. She's put on fifty pounds. There're a lot more wrinkles. There are a lot more gray hairs. Maybe she's not as beautiful as she was thirty-five or forty years ago, but darn it, she's my wife and I pledged love and fidelity to her, and I'm going to obey that.' This is the Church for which we were ordained."

I don't know if you're familiar with Carlo Carretto. He's an Italian priest, a poet. Back in 1984, he put out his autobiography, *I Sought and I Found*. Listen to how he writes:

> How much I must criticize you, my church, and yet how much I love you. You have made me suffer and yet I owe more to you than anybody else. You have given me much scandal, and yet you alone have made me understand holiness. Never in this world have I seen anything more compromised, more false, and yet never have I touched anything more pure, more generous, more beautiful. Countless times I have felt like slamming the door of my soul in your face, and yet every night I have prayed that I might die in your sure arms. No, I cannot be free of you for I am one with you. Then, too, where else would I go? *Ad quem ibimus?* To build another church? But I could not build one without the same defects because they happen to be mine. It would then be my church, not yours. No, I'm old enough to know better.

This quote from Carlo Carretto reminds me of a letter I got right after I first came to Milwaukee in the midst of scandals. The letter was from a very haughty couple who wrote:

> Well, we just want to let you know that we have decided to leave the Catholic Church. It is just too corrupt. It's just too scandalous, everything that's gone on in this archdiocese. We've had it. It's a little too tawdry for us. We are going to find a much more acceptable and a much more perfect church.

I shouldn't be proud of this, but I wrote back and I said, "Well, good luck. And if you find one, don't join it, because then it won't be perfect anymore."

That's what Carretto says, right? Where else would I go? To build another church? Well, it would have the same defects because they're mine, and then it wouldn't be His Church, it'd be mine.

THE CRUCIFIED CHURCH

In the year 2000, I was asked by the Congregation for Catholic Education to host a meeting of all the seminary rectors in Europe for the Jubilee Year. I asked Archbishop Giuseppe Pittau, at the time the Secretary for the Congregation for Catholic Education, to give the keynote address. I told him, "The theme is, 'What our seminarians need to hear today' — what we as rectors need, the lesson that we as rectors need to teach our seminaries most today."

Giuseppe Pittau was a Jesuit. He had been *rector magnificus* of Rome's Gregorian University. I figured he might teach the necessity of a strong interior life or the value of a rigorous academic, theological preparation. Instead he told us, "You must teach your men to love the Church. Teach them to love the Church. Without that, they cannot be good, effective priests."

Pope John Paul II said to seminarians and priests in New York, "The wisdom of the Cross is at the heart of the life and ministry of the priest." And sometimes, our love of the Church brings that.

So, we know from experience at times the Church is stunningly beautiful; she is the bride with whom we have hopelessly head-over-heels fallen in love. At other times, we see her warts, her face all covered in Noxzema, her hair in curlers, and yet we love her all the same.

Some think that our Church is too old and wrinkled, too out of it. She needs serious change in such things as her sexual morality and her thinking about women priests. She needs a cleansing of this patriarchal caste system. Others think our Church too young and brash, having wavered on doctrine, too tolerant of heresy, too quick to accommodate the whims of the world. The love that we bear for Jesus and His Church is not always going to be carefree and satisfying, that's for sure. It's going to entail sacrifice and frustration and suffering.

At a World Youth Day, John Paul II made this request:

> I should like to ask you, dear young people, a favor. Be patient with the Church. The Church is always a community of weak and imperfect individuals. God has placed His work of salvation, His plans and His desires in human hands. This is a great risk, but there is no other church than the one founded by Christ. He wants us human beings to be His collaborators in the world and in the Church with all our deficiencies and shortcomings.

Bishop Richard Sklba, Auxiliary Bishop of Milwaukee, tells a story about a beautiful old country church that had to be closed, a wooden church more than a century old. The people there were sad to see it go, although they knew the decision made sense because there was another parish less than five miles down the road, and only a few families were left still worshiping at the old church. So the Archbishop at the time met with the people and said, "When you all decide what you want to do with the old church [building], come back and we'll discuss it."

After some time, the people got back to the archbishop.

"Look," they said, "we don't want to leave the structure up, because people are going to throw rocks at the windows, and we're sure that the building would be vandalized. We don't want to sell the building, because Lord knows it's going to end up an antique shop, or some other church will buy it. So we would like to burn it. We think that would just be a good sign."

And so, Bishop Sklba went out one Saturday night and celebrated a final Mass, with tears all around. Then, once all the sacred articles and whatever else the people could salvage were removed, sure enough, the volunteer fire department came and burned it. Bishop Sklba said it was such a huge bonfire that they all had to step back, so great was the heat. They watched it burn, and they left. Since it was a long ride back, Bishop Sklba spent that night in the area and the next morning, on his way back to the city, he decided to stop by the site.

The church had burned to the ground, leaving just a smoldering pile of ashes. Then, the bishop saw people with buckets of water, making their way through the ruins to pick up the only thing that was left — stacks of nails. Big, huge nails.

Because the fire burned so evenly, as it went down, the nails ended up in neat stacks around the foundation. So the church people were going around with asbestos gloves, taking the nails and dropping them in buckets of water to save them as mementoes.

Bishop Sklba said he was moved to tears as he looked at that foundation and those nails. "Those are the nails that held this church structure together for 125 years," he found himself remembering. And then, it dawned on all present that, as a matter of fact, nails are what usually holds the Church together: the nails of Christ, the wounds of Christ. That means suffering, that means pain, that means blood, that means wounds, that means death . . . but this is the Church that we love.

Again, Flannery O'Connor:

> To have the church be what you want it to be would require the continuous, miraculous meddling of God in human affairs, whereas it is our dignity that we are allowed by God, more or less, to get on with those graces that come through faith and the sacraments, and which work through our human nature. Human nature is so faulty that it can resist any amount of grace and most of the time it does. The church does well to hold her own. You can hardly ask her to show a profit.

Remember Henri de Lubac, the French theologian? He said:

> For what could I know of him without her? She may appear weak, her growth compromised, her means of action ridiculous, her witness too often hidden. Her children may not understand her, but at such a time I shall look at the humiliated face of my spouse and I shall love her all the more, for while some are hypnotized by those features which make her look old, love will make me discover her hidden forces, the silent activity that gives her perpetual youth.

"For what could I know of Him without her?"

Jesus and His Church ask us, "Will you leave Me, too?" And with St. Peter, we reply, "Lord, to whom else shall we go? You and Your Church alone have the words of everlasting life."

Afterword

Neither Silver Nor Gold

Now Peter and John were going up to the temple at the hour of prayer, the ninth hour. And a man lame from birth was being carried, whom they laid daily at that gate of the temple which is called Beautiful to ask alms of those who entered the temple. Seeing Peter and John about to go into the temple, he asked for alms. And Peter directed his gaze at him, with John, and said, "Look at us." And he fixed his attention upon them, expecting to receive something from them. But Peter said, "I have no silver and gold, but I give you what I have; in the name of Jesus Christ of Nazareth, walk." And he took him by the right hand and raised him up; and immediately his feet and ankles were made strong. And leaping up he stood and walked and entered the temple with them, walking and leaping and praising God. And all the people saw him walking and praising God, and recognized him as the one who sat for alms at the Beautiful Gate of the temple; and they were filled with wonder and amazement at what had happened to him.

— Acts 3:1-10

THE PEARL OF GREAT PRICE

I chose that passage from the Acts of the Apostles for this last episode in our consideration of St. Peter because I think it's a good way to sum up his life, the man who has guided us in our meditations in this book. Simply put, it all comes down to Christ. In the end it all comes down to Peter's relationship with Our Lord and Savior, Jesus Christ. What Peter comes to realize, and I presume it's only after the transforming grace of Pentecost, is that Jesus Christ is his greatest treasure. Jesus Christ — to use the words of sacred Scripture — Jesus Christ is indeed his pearl of great price. He has no one else. He wants no one else. He knows no one else. And not only does he have Jesus Christ as his pearl of great price, it is his passion to give this Christ away to others. It is a question of the utter centrality of Jesus. Peter learned the lesson well, and we see him now transformed.

This episode from the early Church, found in the Acts of the Apostles, is a good illustration of where we are as the Church today. In our contemporary circumstances, we really have nothing left in the Church except Jesus Christ. We are reduced to saying with Peter, "We don't have silver and gold, but what we do have we give you willingly. In the name of Jesus Christ, stand up and walk." Maybe we're not *reduced* to that, though, so much as *elevated* to that. It may not be all that bad a place to be.

About three months ago, something startling happened to me. I had a visiting missionary Franciscan bishop, from a terribly poor area of Ecuador, who came to see me — guess why? Now, you know why missionary bishops usually come to see American bishops. But this time, this bishop from Ecuador had a different message for me.

"Archbishop," he said, "I come to visit *you*. You and the Archdiocese in Milwaukee have been so good to us in the past, and now maybe we can help you. Maybe I can share some priests and sisters with you. I don't have any money, but we have strong faith and I am blessed with vocations. Maybe I can share that with you. Maybe you would like to come and relax for a while. I have a simple home, but it is beautiful, and it's cool in the mountains. You could come and relax, or maybe some of your priests would like to come here . . ." And so he went on and on.

It used to be that bishops would come to us for silver and gold, but this bishop — what he's telling me is, "My brother, Timothy, I know you don't have silver and gold. I know you don't even have the prestige and the prominence that bishops and priests used to have. So maybe we could help you." This was a grace for me. Is it for you? That's where we're at in the Church in the United States, and maybe it's not such a bad thing.

Maybe it's not such a bad thing that, because of all the upheaval, all the scandals, all the shortages of priests, all the lawsuits, and everything else that's gone on the last forty tumultuous years, we don't have silver and gold anymore. We can barely pay our bills. But what we've got, we're clinging to: the pearl of great price, the most priceless treasure of all, Jesus Christ. And if all this disgrace, and sadness, and shock of the last four decades — all the turmoil that we've gone through in the Church — if that has driven home the centrality, the utter centrality of Jesus, maybe it's not such a bad thing.

NEITHER SILVER NOR GOLD

When I think back to what attracted me to the priesthood, it was that I sensed a call from Jesus to serve Him and His Church. I know that supernatural element was there. But I also have to admit that there was some "glitter" about that call. The first color television I ever saw in my life was — guess where? In the rectory of my parish. The first centrally air-conditioned house I ever entered was in — guess where? The rectory of my parish. The two people who drove the nicest cars in my neighborhood were — guess who? The pastor and the associate. There was glitter!

The priests were men of clout, prestige, and prominence. I'm not saying that's all they were — they were wonderful men and effective priests, as well. They had a deep impact on me because of their faith and their zeal for souls. But that glitter also was there, and that glitter isn't there anymore, is it?

People drive nicer cars than priests do. People have more money than we do. People have more prestige and clout than we do. In fact, sometimes they are embarrassed or ashamed to be around us. Lord knows we don't have any silver and gold. It used to be that people would line up outside a bishop's office for money; now, they know that's not the place to look for it. There isn't any.

We can mourn that; we can cry about that; we can regret that. But I'm wondering if, after all, this isn't in fact a blessed return to the infant Church, where we say with St. Peter, "Silver and gold we don't have, but guess what we do have? The greatest treasure of all, Our Lord and Savior, Jesus Christ, and that we are never going to rest until we can share Him with others."

So it all comes down to the utter centrality of Jesus Christ. We have Him. We have our faith in Him. We have the power of our prayer to Him. We have His presence in His Holy Word. We have His presence in the sacraments, especially the Holy Eucharist. We have the power of His grace and mercy. We have the teaching and preaching of the Church. We have His presence — His gracious presence in the arms of His Blessed Mother, and His presence with us in His people, especially in the poor, the sick, and those who look to us for comfort and direction. That's our treasure. And we don't need any other clutter, any other distraction. Silver and gold we don't have, but we have Jesus Christ, and that's all we need, because He is the pearl of great price.

Reminding ourselves of the utter centrality of Jesus is important. Peter learned it, didn't he? We see it in the Acts of the Apostles, and that's why I love all these different aspirations and sayings and prayers of St. Peter that we've been meditating upon in this book.

During the day, I copy St. Peter; I ape him, in my attempt to ensure the utter centrality of Jesus Christ. So in the morning, when I go down before the Blessed Sacrament, I simply say (as Peter did at the Transfiguration), "Lord, it is good to be here with you."

As I begin the day, as an act of morning offering, or as I begin any project, I'll say, "Lord, if it is really you, tell me to come to you across the water." I can interpret that as an invitation from Jesus to trust Him and to walk on the water toward Him.

When I get nervous, scared, overwhelmed, or tense — and there are so many temptations to do that now — I'll call out to Jesus, with St. Peter, "Save me, Lord. I'm going to drown."

When I'm weighed down by my sin and unworthiness, I will say to Him, "Leave me, Lord, for I am a sinful man."

When I'm yearning for His consolation and His comfort and His presence and His mercy, I will echo St. Peter at the Last Supper: "Lord, wash not only my feet but wash my head and my hands, as well."

When I find myself fatigued and discouraged — and really, I'm just too tired or too distracted to pray, especially at night — I'll simply join St. Peter on the shores of the Sea of Galilee and say, "Lord, you know everything. You know that I love you. Let's just leave it at that."

At times when I'm confused and have difficulty trying to understand His ways, His message, and His will, I'll say, "Lord, to whom shall I go? You and you alone have the words of everlasting life."

When I'm worried about what I have to give people, and what the Church has to do for people, and what the archdiocese can do to minister to people, I say with St. Peter at temple square, "Silver and gold we don't have, but what we have we give. In the name of Jesus Christ, stand up and walk." The utter centrality of Jesus — it all is about Him!

Whenever I make a retreat, I keep a little journal, taking some notes from the conferences, and at the end I'll make some resolutions. Guess what? I can almost put "ditto" on every sheet, because if I look back over the past thirty years, I'm probably making the same resolutions. It drives me nuts. I'm probably having the same regrets, I'm tackling the same sins, and I'm worried about the same temptations. Well, we need not get discouraged.

Quo Vadis?

We have been looking at St. Peter throughout this book, and lessons we learn from his life drawn from the Holy Scriptures. This incident about St. Peter doesn't come from the Gospel, but it is an ancient Christian tradition, and it keeps us from discouragement. You've probably heard it.

Peter, the first Pope, bishop of Rome in the mid-60s AD, is in Rome. The vicious Emperor Nero burns part of the city and decides to blame it on the Christians. Nero orders the Christians to be arrested. So, the Christians are being rounded up throughout Rome. Of course, the prize is going to be Peter, the leader, the shepherd, the pastor of this Christian community.

Peter resorts to his old habits, gets cowardly, and runs out of town. But as he is leaving to avoid the cross and is running out the Appian Way, he goes through the city walls — and who does he meet? The Lord Jesus! He meets Jesus, walking into Rome.

Peter says, "*Domine, quo vadis?*" "Lord, where are You going?"

Jesus looks at Peter and answers, "I'm going back to Rome to be crucified again with My people."

Whereupon Peter turns around and goes back through the Appian Gate, whereupon he is arrested and dragged to a hill across the Tiber called the Vatican, to be crucified upside-down.

It was then, hanging on that cross upside-down, I'm sure, that Peter remembered the time he tried to talk Our Lord out of the cross, and what Jesus had said: "Get behind Me, Satan. You are thinking like a man, not God. Unless you take up your cross and follow Me, you cannot be My disciple." Peter had learned his lesson from the Master.

IN OUR WEAKNESS, WE MEET THE LORD

Peter, of all people, should have known that there was no avoiding the Cross, but he fell again, at that very last minute. And yet it was precisely in his sin, in his weakness, that he met Jesus Christ. So we need never despair in our weakness, for St. Paul reminds us, "My grace is sufficient. My power is made evident in your weakness."

Here is the first lesson that Peter can teach us. We battle the same weaknesses and sins and temptations most of our life. We will up until the end. But we're never discouraged, because it is in those that we meet Jesus Christ and His grace and mercy.

CHRIST IDENTIFIES WITH THE CHURCH

Second, St. Peter learned once again, at this very last moment of his life, that Jesus is identified with His Church. "I am going back to Rome to suffer and be crucified with my Church." Peter learned on the Appian Way what Paul learned on the Road to Damascus: that Jesus and His Church are one.

We, like St. Peter, look to the Church as Christ himself. We look to the Church as the mystical body of Christ, the spotless bride of Christ. We belong to her. We will love her. We pledge our lives to her. We are willing to suffer and die for her. She is beautiful and dazzling and vibrant, yes — but we also know that at times, her members can give her an ugliness of corruption, of frustration and lethargy; we love her all the same.

We never embarrass her. We never give people a reason to leave her. We will always be eager to introduce people to her. We are always ready to sacrifice for her, because she is the love of our life. What could we know of Jesus without her? Love for Jesus and His Church has to be the passion of our lives. This is the second lesson Peter learns and teaches us at the last moment of his life: a love for the Church and a desire to be with the Church, even when she is suffering.

EMBRACING THE PASCHAL MYSTERY

Finally, St. Peter teaches us in this episode to embrace all the more enthusiastically the Paschal mystery. You know what the Paschal mystery is. I can give it tons of definitions. I love Pius Parsch's definition, that the Paschal mystery is the dying and rising of Jesus and our incorporation into it .

You know how the story ends, of course. The story doesn't end with Peter being embarrassed on the Appian Way. The story ends that Peter is once again enchanted, captivated, renewed, converted by Jesus Christ. He turns around, returns to Rome, is arrested, and is dragged to the Vatican Hill. There, the tormentors say, "You are so in love with this guy Jesus, we'll put you to death the same way we put Him to death. Get ready to be crucified." Whereupon he asks, "Please, please, crucify me upside-down. I'm not worthy. I'm not worthy to die the way He did."

There he is: literally, his world is upside-down because of Jesus Christ. And what seems the moment of degradation and death — his martyrdom — Peter knows is instead a moment of triumph and resurrection, because the world's values are turned upside-down as he is turned that way on the cross.

After his horrible death, later that night — when the soldiers are all passed out from wine — do the remaining surviving Christians come and take his body and walk it about the length of two football fields away to that pagan necropolis. There, they bury his body; they know where it is; from that day, it becomes the center of clandestine pilgrimages, until at last Constantine erects a magnificent temple there in the first part of the fourth century. Today, on that spot rises the church that symbolizes Christendom — almost a physical realization to the prophecy of Jesus that "upon this rock I will build my church." It is literally above the body of St. Peter that the church of St. Peter rises. It's an icon of the Paschal mystery that in Peter's sin, Peter's conversion, and Peter's martyrdom, life comes. It's also a figure of the dying and rising of Jesus and our incorporation into it: unless the grain of wheat fall to the ground and die, it just remains a grain of wheat. But once it dies, it brings about new life.

All of St. Peter's life was the Paschal mystery. Dying to self, to selfishness, to stupidity, to pride, to stubbornness, to cowardice, and rising again to new life, conformed to Jesus

Christ. On the Appian Way, he dies once again to his sin — his self-preservation — and then is crucified. He crucifies himself, his old self, to the cross and rises again with Jesus Christ.

So do we, every single day that we're called to be absorbed into the dying and rising of Jesus. Our everyday sins, temptations, struggles, agonies, sufferings, failures — they're just an invitation to die with Christ and rise again with him.

Walter Burghardt, S.J, the celebrated Jesuit preacher, says the words that Jesus used at the Last Supper to institute the Eucharist — those words that we hear every day in the Eucharistic prayer — that is what Jesus wants to do with us. He took the bread, He blessed it, He broke it, He gave it. That's what He does to us. He taks us, He blesses us, He breaks us, and then He gives us to others.

Daily, we're called to that cycle of dying and rising. It's never over. We do not want it to be. Isn't that the interpretive key to understanding the ups and downs, the ins and outs, the sin and the grace of our Christian lives? Daily dying and rising with Jesus . . .

Like Peter.